Around the World
in 80 Lays

Around the World in 80 Lays

Adventures in Sex Travel

Joe Diamond

Skyhorse Publishing

To Lonnie Hanover, who enjoys life as much as anyone I know.

Skyhorse Publishing books may be purchased in bulk at special discounts for sales promotion, corporate gifts, fund raising, or educational purposes. Special editions can also be created to specifications. For details, contact the Special Sales Department, Skyhorse Publishing, 555 Eighth Avenue, Suite 903, New York, NY 10018 or info@skyhorsepublishing.com.

www.skyhorsepublishing.com

10 9 8 7 6 5 4 3 2 1

Library of Congress Cataloging-in-Publication Data

Diamond, Joe, 1964-
Around the world in 80 lays : adventures in sex travel / Joe Diamond.
p. cm.
ISBN 978-1-60239-287-8 (alk. paper)
1. Sex tourism. 2. Tourists--Sexual behavior. 3. Travelers--Sexual behavior. 4. Sex-oriented businesses--Social aspects. I. Title. II. Title: Around the world in eighty lays.
HQ117.D53 2008
306.87409'051--dc22
2008026550

Printed in the United States of America

CONTENTS

Author's Note

Under threat of having my balls pushed out through my throat, I've made judicious use of pseudonyms throughout the book to protect both the innocent and the not-so-innocent. Otherwise, every word of this narrative is true.

Introduction

AS AN INTRODUCTION, I'D LIKE TO POINT OUT THAT THE PHRASE
"eighty lays" doesn't do me any justice. It's been many more than
eighty. I lost count long ago. I've paid for sex all over the world,
paid for blondes and brunettes, paid for full-time sluts and part-
time college students. I've paid for more threesomes than I can
count. For as little as sixty bucks a night, I've fucked my way across
the globe: Brazil, the Dominican Republic, Costa Rica, Vegas. I've
financed my sexcapades with a little porn journalism for *Hustler*
and other skin mags on the side. Within these pages you'll see the
life of a self-described *whoremonger*, and I hope you enjoy it.

As an added bonus, I've included the juicy experiences of some
of my mongering friends—because no matter how hard I try, I can't
do it all.

Though all of my eighty (plus!) lays were with willing adult
participants, each woman was wildly different from the next. Some
of the girls liked me; some of them probably loathed me. Some
kissed me on the lips and held my hand, while others ripped me

off or straight up robbed me. Some just wanted a seemingly rich American boyfriend to take them shopping. Some wanted to cuddle and talk about their problems, and others just wanted to suck me off and move on to the next customer. They're all here—Daniela, Antoinette, Juliana, Jessie, Betina, Estela, Tina, Luciana . . .

I should really start keeping a list.

I should also note that while I've traveled the world for sex, these pages concentrate heavily on my experiences in Latin America. This is where I first began mongering, and it's still my favorite place to monger. The women are sexy, the air is sultry, and I know exactly where to go to get exactly what I want. I've been robbed, ripped off, and had my heart broken, and yet I always go back for more. Sex is a way of life down there. Prostitution is legal. It's out in the open and on practically every street corner. Down there, I can find a *Pretty Woman* almost every night. And I'm no Richard Gere. Someday, maybe I'll become a *sexpat* and retire to Brazil, living the life of other Western men who tired of just having *fuckations* and wanted the mongering lifestyle year-round. But for now, I travel and pay for sex as often as I can.

So why me? How did a guy who started as an orthodox Jewish yeshiva boy, who went on to work for law-and-order crusader Rudy Giuliani, and who then carved out his own niche as an anti-crime advocate become an out-and-out hedonist? I'm still a conservative on everything from the death penalty to national security, but when it comes to sex between consenting adults—whether money's involved or not—I'm more Howard Stern than Pat Robertson.

Sex with no strings attached. Sex with beautiful women. Sex without the possibility of rejection. Hello?! I can spend months at the bars in Manhattan and never come close to getting laid. As a monger, a couple of hours after my plane takes off, I can be getting off with a tanned *garota* who likes my American accent.

Finally, we mongers have our own language, and our own secret codes, so for all you "civilians" reading these pages, get ready to learn a thing or two about the world. Maybe you'll love the stories because you can live vicariously through them. You might know that mongering isn't really a possibility for you, but secretly you wish it was. So the next best thing is to hear our tales. I don't advocate this lifestyle to everyone, and I'm no poster boy for some kind of sexual revolution. But this much I know: I'm not alone.

—Joe Diamond

CHAPTER ONE

Hurricane Juliana

UNTIL MY FIRST TRIP THERE IN MARCH OF 2003, I HAD THREE images of Rio de Janeiro in my mind: Carnival debauchery, the huge statue of Christ, and pristine beaches whose names I didn't know. Copacabana, to me, was a Barry Manilow song. I also knew the song "Girl from Ipanema," but I didn't know it referred to a beach in Rio. Half the time I'd confuse Rio with Buenos Aires, Argentina.

It was Ian who'd paved my way, bombarding me and his other friends with emails about the prostitutes he'd met abroad. He'd go to Latin America every few months. Then he'd work himself into a funk comparing his ease overseas at finding a *Girlfriend Experience* (GFE) to his lack of success with American women. "They treat you like a king in Rio," he'd tell us. "Of course they do," we'd snicker. "You're paying them to." We'd tell him that there was nothing wrong with enjoying himself while on vacation, but that he had to stop living there in his mind when he was home. He needed to push himself more to meet women in New York.

As if I were qualified to preach on the topic. I'd screwed up all of my major relationships, and now I was having a rough time even getting dates. But dry spell or not, I liked going out, and after a few beers, I enjoyed the challenge of approaching women. If one could compile a scorecard of these approaches since I'd started going out in my late teens, the number of rejections would no doubt be staggering. Still, I'd met most of the girls I'd dated—including the three I'd come closest to marrying—in the nightclubs and bars of New York City and its suburbs. But now, I was in my late thirties and, like Ian, I was wondering what the hell I had to show for it.

Ian would often urge me to travel with him to Brazil. But no matter how lonely I felt, I still couldn't justify taking a ten-hour flight to purchase sex. I didn't even do that at home, unless you counted buying porn. I'd gone with a hooker once—a friend bought me a hand job by the West Side Highway for my eighteenth birthday. She had fingers like sandpaper, which was just as well, because the AIDS epidemic was just getting underway in America, and the last thing I needed was to develop a taste for the ladies of the night.

So to me, there were two types of prostitutes: disease-ridden, drug-addled streetwalkers who couldn't pay me to sleep with them, and gorgeous call girls who were beyond the limits of my bank account.

Ian claimed that Rio's *garotas de programa* ("program girls," Brazilian slang for prostitutes, in honor of their having a schedule, or program, of appointments with clients) occupied a magic middle ground: call girl quality at streetwalker prices. But I still wasn't sold. Pursuing women was as much about validation as sex. What good would paying for it do? Was that the only way I could get laid? If anything, I thought it would make me feel more disgusted with myself.

"GFE," was Ian's mantra. "If she likes you, it's almost like dating," he said. "She'll see you when she's not working. Shit, she'll travel with you around the country if you want."

"You still pay the girls for their time, right?"

"Depends how much they like you. You take them out to eat, of course. And they love presents. Clothes, toys for their kids, little knick-knacks." Ian would scour the cheap gift shops in Manhattan's Chinatown before a trip to Rio and load up on junk for the garotas.

I was sure there was more than a bit of self-delusion in Ian's glowing depiction of Rio. But I'd been thinking about going to New Orleans for Mardi Gras, and Ian's obsession with Rio got me thinking about Carnival. The Catholic holiday right before Lent, Carnival comes from a Latin phrase that essentially means "last chance for meat." But seeing as it has evolved into one of the wildest festivals on the globe, it's probably no longer the kind of flesh fest that the Church had in mind.

Like Ian, I initially saw Carnival as an opportunity to meet "normal" women—tourists or locals fired up by the anything-goes atmosphere.

I got a good deal at the Guanabara Palace, a hotel in Centro, Rio's business district. Ian had arrived in town two days before me, and was staying in an apartment in Copacabana.

I phoned him after I checked in. As if he'd been sitting by the phone for hours, obsessing over the opportunity to take me to Help Discoteca, Rio's hooker central and his favorite stomping ground, the first thing out of his mouth was "We have to go to Help tonight."

"Hooker heaven, right?" I asked.

"Say *garotas*. It sounds better."

"You don't understand," I said. "It's my first night. I want to meet regular girls."

"Joe, everything's open all night. We'll go to Help for a little while, then somewhere else."

I took a bus to Avenida Atlantica and walked toward Help's yellow neon sign, about a quarter-mile ahead. As I passed by the Marriott and other large hotels, I noticed that the weather was comfortable, though it was the height of Brazilian summer. It felt like New York City in May, but without the brutal tropical humidity I'd expected.

The sidewalk in front of Help Discoteca was a thicket of street commerce: old women selling beers from Styrofoam coolers; barefoot kids waving gum and cigarettes in my face or thrusting out their hands for money; teens with shoe-shine boxes. Ian had warned me about those. I spotted Ian and we got on line. Help was set way back from the street, and the line stretched nearly to the curb.

I scanned the crowd, surprised, despite what Ian had told me, by the lack of girls dressed trashy-sexy, like streetwalkers do in the States. There were a few like that, sure, but most—in tight skirts, high heels, and belly shirts—were dressed no more provocatively than girls in any large city out for a night of partying. Some of the girls were beautiful, but a greater number were just attractive—again, just like in any big club. I had yet to fall under Rio's reputed spell.

"You sure they're prostitutes?" I asked Ian.

"I told you," he said. "The garotas look like college girls."

"Most of these girls are not garotas. They can't be."

"Ninety-nine percent. At least. I know, because I've been with lots of the girls here."

The walls inside Help were a canopy of metallic blue discs. As we headed to the bar, Ian pointed to the love seats on the catwalk above. "That's where you get to test-drive the girls a bit."

I had my first caipirinha, Brazil's national cocktail. It tasted like crap, but its cachaça (a liquor similar to rum) was strong enough to give me the quick buzz I wanted. Now everyone became more alluring. As I watched the garotas gyrate to samba and other Latin rhythms, I started to understand why *Brasileiras* are widely considered the sexiest women on earth.

I often get an exaggerated sense of power when alcohol first hits me, and I got it in my head that I could score with these girls without "tainting" the achievement by paying them. Hookers or not, they were still human and would be susceptible to my charms, I foolishly reasoned.

Not quite! I approached six or seven girls, none of whom fell for my charms. Getting rejected by any girl stings. But a prostitute? It's an exquisite form of devastation, like getting slammed in the balls with a Louisville Slugger. What the hell was I doing here?

Eventually, I'd figure out that Help's garotas have a sixth sense about men who don't intend to honor the rules. And the cardinal rule, of course, is no pay, no play.

I went back to Ian, who had settled in by the bar. He was already holding hands with a petite brunette. She was smiling at him, hardly noticing me. "This is Silvia," Ian said. "Remember? I emailed you her photo."

He'd emailed it about a thousand times. Ian had this habit of repeatedly clicking the send button. Not only that, but he'd sent it to all of my email addresses—home, work, etc., just to make sure I got it.

"We're going," Ian said. "Are you okay?"

"Where are we going?"

"No, I'm leaving with Silvia. Is that okay?"

"Yeah. When are you coming back?"

Ian chuckled. "Not tonight. Stay here as long as you want. You're in fucking Paradise now."

I still had doubts about that, but I kept them to myself.

"Just make sure you take a cab to your hotel," Ian said. "Don't take a bus this late. I'll call you tomorrow?"

"Sure," I said. I was angry, but I wasn't about to make Ian my babysitter.

I had enough of Help, though. I left the club and wandered through Terraco Atlantico, the sidewalk café next door. It was teeming with garotas. But they were friendlier, or at least more aggressive, than the ones in Help. "Hey, baby," a girl said as she grabbed my crotch. "To where you wanna go?" This was more like it. Her friend also rubbed my fly. "*Safado*," she cooed. Brazilian hookers were always calling gringos "safado," which literally means "shameless." It's slang for a super-horny motherfucker who can't keep his dick in his pants. Depending on the context "safado" could be high praise, meaning that you're a sex machine who they'd adore having between their legs. Other times it was a garota's way of calling you a cheating bastard who just wants to screw everything that moves.

This particular garota was one of the girls who'd blown me off in Help. *Fuck you,* I felt like saying. *You had your chance.*

I made my way toward a pair of girls sitting near the hedges. One of the girls had light-brown hair and a silk blouse with diagonal black and pink stripes. She smiled. "American?"

I nodded. "New York."

She introduced herself as Antoinette and asked me to sit. Her friend was tired and left after a few minutes. I was amazed at how well Antoinette spoke English. She seemed awfully poised for a working girl, and looked thirty-two or thirty-three, older than most of the garotas I'd seen that night. Maybe she was just in town for Carnival, and I'd stumbled onto a chance for legitimate romance. In the hopes of preserving that chance, I stopped myself from asking straight off if she was "working."

The more we spoke, the more turned on I got. She was from São Paulo, where she owned a beauty parlor and taught dancing. She had a three-year-old daughter whom she couldn't wait to get back to. Now and then, Antoinette would sprinkle our conversation with Portuguese to help me practice.

"*E você?*" she asked.

"Wait. I know what that means—*And you.*"

"*Perfeito!* What do you do?"

I was working at the time for an advocacy group that fought for tougher laws against crime. "We need that here," Antoinette said. "Crime in Brazil is terrible."

A chunky man with his arms around a blonde and a brunette waddled by on the sidewalk just beyond the hedges. He barely came up to his dates' chins, and his toupee kept kicking up in the ocean wind. This didn't dampen the girls' apparent zeal for leaning over and kissing him on the mouth, though.

Meanwhile, a muscular young American at the next table told his friends, "I did one of those girls last night." His pals high-fived him. Maybe "doing business" with the garotas wasn't so bad. Everyone seemed into it, even these jock-types who I imagined had no problem getting laid back home.

I was beginning to feel more relaxed about being in Rio, and hoped that Antoinette would make an encouraging gesture, like touching my knee or cheek. But she limited things to conversation. Soon, though, she moved her chair closer ("Is this okay?" she asked), and brushed my hair back with her fingers. "I can see your eyes better now."

"Do you want to. . . um . . . ?" I asked.

"Yes, Joe?"

"Um . . . go somewhere?"

She smiled. "Go where?"

"I feel weird asking you, but to my hotel."

"This is possible."

I still wasn't sure what was going on. Were we talking business, or was Antoinette genuinely attracted to me?

"I need to ask you something first, and I hope you won't be offended," I said.

"Yes?" She had a knowing grin.

"It's just that, given where we are, with all the garotas and . . . "

She held her finger to my mouth. "Yes, Joe. I come to Rio to make program."

"But you don't seem like the other girls here."

"I only do this for Carnival and the New Year's," she explained. "Or when I have a client in Rio."

Antoinette said that most work in Brazil, even owning your own business, paid shit. She made more money in a few weeks as a prostitute than at her other jobs the rest of the year.

"I've never been with a garota," I said. "Do we talk money first?"

"If you want. Or we can do that later. In the morning."

"But what if I don't have enough?"

She played with my hair again. "You worry about everything, don't you?" she said. "If I was only concerned about making the most money, I would not have relaxed here with you all this time. This is your *primeira vez*—'first time'—in Rio. All you should think about is enjoying it."

Back at the hotel, it was impossible not to enjoy it. Antoinette peeled off her blouse to reveal a flat tummy and small, beautifully shaped breasts. Can breasts have personality? They seemed perky as hell when Antoinette was bouncing on me. Bouncing, like a kid on a trampoline, deliriously happy.

In the morning, she asked what I wanted to pay.

"Is $60 good?" I meant it just as an opening bid, and was stunned that she accepted it without negotiation.

Ian would later tell me that he was also surprised: "Most of the girls by Help want to bang out a deal as soon as they meet you. They ask for '$200 American,' which is insane, and they know it. Then you laugh at them—but warmly, as if you know they're joking—and say, '$200? I'll give you $40.'"

"For a whole night? Shit!" I said. "I paid too much."

"No, forty is low," Ian explained. "Remember, you're negotiating. Usually, it'll end up somewhere between $60 and $100. But your girl didn't even try to bargain. She's probably counting on you for repeat business. As well as gifts, dinner."

"She's well worth it," I said. "She's incredible."

"I told you," Ian responded. "You've got the bug."

He was right, too. Antoinette had ended my aversion to prostitutes. The transaction hadn't made me feel at all like a loser. Instead, she had lifted the curtain on a sexual Disney World. Sure, I'd had to pay. But for one of the most thrilling encounters of my life. And there were countless attractions here yet to explore.

* * * *

Quatro por Quatro, Rio's largest brothel, was three blocks from my hotel. It was on the middle of a quiet side street, just off one of Rio's main commercial strips. Gringos loved the place; its location and afternoon opening time also made it a favorite among local businessmen out for lunchtime diversions. For a renowned pleasure palace, it had the most pedestrian of names. "Quatro por quatro" literally means "four by four," after the brothel's address, 44 Rua Buenos Aires.

I went there my third day in Rio. As much as I wanted to dash in and look at the girls, I had to follow a protocol that's standard in most *termas*, Rio's upscale brothels. First, I checked in at reception, where a pretty Asian explained in fluent English the price for one girl versus two, forty minutes versus an hour, and small rooms versus deluxe ones. "You decide later, after you pick a girl," she said. She handed me a key on a wristband and pointed me to a locker room. As I got closer, a vague scent I'd noticed upon entering the brothel—Lemon Pledge meets steambath—got stronger.

The attendant gave me mandatory gear: sandals and a white robe emblazoned with Quatro por Quatro's logo. After you change, you can go upstairs and take a sauna, shower, or massage. Or you can do what I did: head for the brothel's little nightclub, where clients and garotas size each other up.

The room was packed with Brazilian eye candy in thongs and lingerie. A few were stripping on the small stage. There were some uncomfortable-looking men sitting on black leather couches against mirrored walls. I was too self-conscious to begin flirting, so I showed the bartender my key (all charges are billed to your locker number) and ordered a beer. A tall girl pinched my ass and tried to make chitchat, but I was still adjusting to the new terrain and paid her little mind.

I bought another beer and planted myself at an empty table. Two blondes swooped down on me. One spoke passable English. Almost immediately, she asked if I wanted a threesome. This was always my fantasy. I found the girls moderately appealing; they even kissed briefly to tease me. But Antoinette had spoiled me the way she had taken her time flirting, slowly building my adrenaline. These two seemed like typical quick-buck artists. And not very artful at that. They showed little flair for seduction.

I excused myself to go to the bathroom. But I only made it a few steps before I was mesmerized by an olive-skinned girl swaying at the edge of the dance floor. Her straight blonde hair (Quatro por Quatro is known as a temple for blonde fetishists) fell just below her shoulders. Even in heels, she didn't seem much taller than me—a bonus for an insecure short guy in a strange environment.

She looked worldly and innocent at the same time. A woman-child. But the more I studied her, the more provocative she seemed. She had on a bright-red thong, and a bikini that strained to rein in her breasts. She had a nice butterfly tattoo across her lower back. But a disturbing line of red dots went from her neck to a small sun tattoo above her breast. A skin condition? Something worse? (She'd later tell me the dots were a sunbeam, but I wasn't entirely convinced. If she was telling the truth, the tattoo artist needed to have his hands broken so he could never repeat such an aesthetic atrocity.)

When she noticed me staring at her, she locked eyes on mine, came over and stroked my cheek. "*Swah-vay*," she purred Portuguese for "soft." Without another word, she threw her arms around me and kissed me. There's a scene in *West Side Story* where Tony and Maria see each other for the first time across the dance floor. Everything around them fades as they move toward each other, inexorably, like two sleepwalkers. This kiss felt that way. This was no gradual flirtation as it had been with Antoinette. No. This garota had me trembling from the start.

She told me her name was Juliana and quickly led me out of the nightclub to a spiral staircase. As we climbed up, the girl who'd proposed the threesome to me was coming down. "Fucking asshole," she screamed at me as she passed. Nothing personal, I wanted to tell her. But her vehemence was so over the top, I almost fell down the stairs laughing. My ego was inflating. Was it really this easy? All those wasted nights I spent getting rejected by beautiful American women—and here I was with two women fighting over who was going to fuck me?

When we reached the empty lounge at the top, I told her that I'd more-or-less rejected that other girl for her. She pulled me onto a couch and kissed me again.

Here was the "simplicity" of Rio. Your goal, if it merely involved hot sex, was always pretty much within reach. If you wanted something more, like a GFE sprinkled with a fantasy of intimacy (*fantamacy*, as I like to call it), you could have that too. It was a conveniently fleeting intimacy that didn't threaten to interfere with your actual life, like a hot dream right before the alarm clock rings. It had all the benefits of intimacy without any of the drawbacks. Perfect for a commitment-phobe like me.

Every so often, Juliana and I would try to overcome the language barrier and have a sustained conversation. I pieced together that she had a little boy and girl. Their father was out of the picture, and Juliana wasn't in a relationship. I wanted to learn more about her, but for now I just wanted to keep kissing. The fact that we could get a room and fuck wasn't important. I would have been happy all night with her on that couch, just embracing. She seemed to feel the same way, making no attempt to sell me on a session, which was the only way terma girls made money.

I'd occasionally sneak a peek in the mirror behind us, and think, "Joe, you're a really cute guy." It was a nice contrast to the countless times since puberty when I'd look at my reflection and home in on my acne. Or large nostrils. Or puffy eyelids. No wonder those girls blew me off, I'd think.

We must have been there at least two hours, when finally she said, "Let's go make-a love."

As we headed downstairs, we passed two attractive garotas. Without realizing it, I looked at them a little too long. Juliana glared at me. "You dog," she said.

"I'm sorry," I said. "I want to be with you, not them."

"You dog. Get away from me."

She rushed off to the girls' dressing room. I followed as far as the door, and thought about going in. You'd expect a terma, with its volatile mix of hookers, horny men, and liquor, to have a phalanx of bouncers, but the only security I'd seen was a man at the entrance. Still, I was sure that the place had heavy-duty stealth security, and that if I opened the door to the dressing room I'd be pounded into the floor.

I was oddly elated. Here was a prostitute I'd just met, yet apparently I'd made her so jealous that she'd fled without making a cent. Maybe it was all an act, or maybe she had real feelings for me. Either way, I knew I was smitten.

I needed to make that clear to her. I asked Christina, the receptionist, to translate the phrase "You make my heart stop" to Portuguese. She wrote it on a napkin and practiced with me.

I went back into the nightclub and stood by the door, hoping that Juliana would show. I was rude to an especially clingy garota; how would Juliana react if she saw me talking to another girl? Yet always in the back of my mind, I realized how insane it was to be thinking like this, in a brothel of all places.

I studied the napkin in the dim light. Juliana walked in and pretended not to see me. I apologized again, and carefully spoke my prepared phrase.

"Huh?" she said, looking angrier than before.

Did I botch it? Did it come out sounding like an insult? I convinced her to come with me to reception so I could repeat it away from the noise, with Christina there for backup.

This time Juliana nodded that she understood, although she didn't exactly melt in my arms. She still looked pissed, but she took me back to the lounge. There, she sat with her arms folded and continued to glower.

"I like you so much," I said. "The last thing I wanted to do was upset you." I don't know how much of my English she understood, but I think my earnestness registered.

Juliana was clearly erratic, but it made things more exciting. There was also the possibility that she was a lot shrewder than she seemed, and had manipulated me to the point where I was eagerly kissing her ass. Whatever her motives, she eventually softened. She let me kiss her, and soon things soared to the fever pitch of earlier.

We headed for the cabins. This time I fixed my eyes on her. Other girls popped in and out of view, but my eyes didn't budge.

As she got undressed, Juliana said she didn't want me to fuck her. Other men there fucked her. With me it'd be making love. I wondered how many other guys she'd said it to that day, but I didn't dwell on it. *Just enjoy the fantasy*, I thought. *The return flight to reality and your drab life in Brooklyn is only days away.*

Juliana pushed me down on the small bed, laid down on me and kissed me again, this time grinding her freshly-shaved crotch against me right below my tummy. She stopped to grab a condom from her bag and put it on me. I'd been aroused for hours now, and the thought occurred to me that it might not take much for her to make me come. If I couldn't hold out long enough, I had the feeling I'd lose plenty of stock with her. Obviously, many hookers would be happy just to finish you off as quickly as possible, take their earnings, and move on to the next client. But Juliana had invested a lot of time in me that day, and it was late enough where she probably wouldn't have time to hook up with new clients. So I don't think she would have been impressed if I'd exploded on contact.

She was teasing me, wiggling her crotch down ever so close to mine. I tried to hold her still before she went in for the kill. She wiggled loose, and slid onto me. Ecstasy. Now it was my turn to tease. I turned her over, and grabbing each of her legs near the knee, I thrust deeply. She shuddered. I pulled my cock out and showed it to her, condom glistening. She reached for it, but I slapped her hand away.

"Is this what you wanted?" I asked, as I slowly reinserted the head of my cock into her dripping wet pussy. "Is this what you were looking for?"

I held that position a moment, then took a few short thrusts before reentering her fully. Then I pulled out and started the whole routine over again: first the head, then a few short thrusts, and then, finally, the whole cock.

This drove her wild. And after doing this three or four times, she grabbed me by the ass as I was pulling out, forcing me to stay buried deep.

"I want it," she said. "Quit teasing me."

I grabbed her by the calf with both hands and turned her over onto her side. Then I eased her onto her knees into the doggy-style position. Just the sight of her in that position, her ass up in the air, her pussy soaked and waiting, was enough to cause me to explode. So I did what any red-blooded American man would do in that situation: I grabbed her by the hips, entered her, and fucked her as hard as I could for as long as I could before climaxing.

I'd like to be able to tell you that this took a half hour. Fifteen minutes, even. But it didn't. In truth, I don't think I made it more than five minutes before I burst. But I fucked her like a man, all right. My second experience as a monger had been a successful one.

Afterward, we cuddled in the lounge. Around closing time, she told me to meet her outside on the corner. First I'd have to get my clothes and pay the bill. *"Rapido! Rapido!"* she said, explaining that she'd have to get home and couldn't wait long. I wasn't sure why she wanted to meet outside, but I hauled ass and did exactly as she said. I went to the corner, and waited. And waited. Another girl from the terma walked by, and I asked if she'd seen Juliana. She said she'd already left. It couldn't be. I'd done everything Juliana said. I lingered a few moments, then drifted in disappointment back to my hotel, wondering where I'd screwed up.

Apparently, I just hadn't moved quickly enough. At least that's what I learned the next night when I returned to Quatro por Quatro, where I found Juliana in the nightclub. She was sitting on a middle-aged man's lap, feeding him french fries. She said something to the man, came over, and kissed me on the cheek. With a sad look, she explained that she'd gone to meet me on the corner as planned and was going to give me her number—but I wasn't there and she'd had to catch her bus.

Now Juliana's current client was shooting impatient looks her way. "Come," she said. I followed her to reception, where she spoke quickly to her friend Christina in Portuguese. She kissed me again and went back inside.

"Joe, she wants to be with you," Christina said. "But the man has already reserved a room."

"No problem," I said. "I'll come back tomorrow."

"Can you wait for her? She'll be free after."

I had plans to meet Ian later for dinner in Copacabana, and I didn't want to hang around.

I joined Ian at Meia Pataca, another outdoor café on Avenida Atlantica, a block away from Help. Meia Pataca is where mongers trade war stories, and the first stop in many garotas' nightly ritual. Around eight, they converge on it, working the tourists for a few hours.

I ripped through four beers with my meal. Ian wouldn't have to hype me on Help tonight. I wanted to get my mind off Juliana, and the best way I could think of was to lose myself with other girls.

We'd just gotten on line for Help when I saw Antoinette, my lucky first lay, on the avenue. "Ian, is it okay if I potentially blow you off?" I asked.

He gave me a thumbs-up.

I caught up with Antoinette on the corner. "Rescue me," I said.

"You are so cute. You've been drinking. Rescue from what?"

"Where are you going?" I asked.

She pointed at Bob's, the fast-food place across the street.

"I'll treat you," I said. "But then you have to bounce on me again."

"So you'll be my dessert. But I must warn you, I am very bouncy tonight."

"Then let's get the food to go."

Antoinette was a great tonic. She made no pretense of emotional involvement. She wasn't going to get into a relationship with anyone until she saved up enough money to start her own dancing school. This didn't stop me from fishing for signs that she might have more than just a professional interest in me, though.

"I could really start to like you," I said.

She wagged her finger. "Joe, you are very sweet and I like your company. But keep your heart out of this. Is that all right?"

"That's fine. But I can still enjoy the fantasy, right? Believe it or not, I'm very romantic."

Around three in the morning, we were watching TV. I had such a strong rapport with her that I asked how much it would cost to "rent" her company, around the clock, for the next four or five days.

"You really want to spend all that time with me?" She started tickling me. "You are crazy."

"Of course I am. So how much?"

"You tell me."

"$500 American, for five whole days."

"$550," she said, "for four days, twenty-three hours, and fifty-nine minutes." Clearly, she was also a fan of *Pretty Woman*. (Lest anyone think I'm obsessed with that film, I also love *The 40-Year-Old Virgin* and *Die Hard 2*.) We tried to seal the deal by having sex, but I wasn't recuperated from the last round.

"You know that Viagra is sold here in every drugstore," she said. "A doctor's permission isn't needed."

"I didn't think I would be having that much sex here."

Thank god I was wrong.

"Tomorrow we'll buy you some." She giggled. "And you can take it off my fee."

We planned to sleep late, then go sightseeing to Sugarloaf Mountain and the statue of Christ on Corcovado Mountain. I'm Jewish, but it still felt somewhat sacrilegious, the idea of going there with a prostitute.

But we were awakened early by a phone call. It was Juliana, saying something about coming to my hotel. Panicking, I kept saying that I didn't understand her. Antoinette asked what was happening. Juliana heard her: "Who is that?"

"It's the television," I said, as I gestured to Antoinette to shut up. Antoinette giggled to herself, but with exaggerated expressions, trying to make me laugh.

I asked Juliana to call back the hotel and ask for Orlando, a young front-desk employee I'd befriended, and give him the information. He'd translate for me. Orlando phoned soon after and said that Juliana was taking the day off and would be at the hotel at eleven thirty.

I told Antoinette. "Poor Joe," she said. "All these women chasing you."

"I don't know what to do now. This girl makes me *loco*, but . . ."

"You care about her, don't you? She's a garota, Joe. Do you know what you're doing?"

"Not a clue. Why would she come here? I swear I didn't make any plans with her."

"She's not stupid. She sees how you feel about her, and she wants to take advantage of another nice American who can afford to stay in a nice hotel."

"I'm not so sure." I told her about Juliana's tantrum at the terma.

"Well, maybe she's crazy. Like you. What do you want to do, then? She's coming here, right?" Antoinette tickled my stomach. "Maybe you can have both of us together."

It was a nice idea, but Juliana seemed more likely to take a machete to my throat than to share me with Antoinette.

"I don't know what to do," I said. Truth is, as much as I liked Antoinette, Juliana was in my blood. "Would you be mad if I took you for breakfast, and then we get together some other time?"

"It's your money, baby. Forget breakfast, just give me my $550 and I'll leave you to your crazy garota."

"Antoinette, that price was for five days, not one night."

"Baby, we agreed. It's not my fault you changed your mind."

I was on the verge of an anxiety attack.

"Relax, Joe. *Eu estou brincando com você*—I am fucking with you."

"Bitch!" I tickled her arm.

God, I loved Rio.

After a quick breakfast in the hotel, I gave Antoinette $100 and thanked her for being so understanding. If I could have transplanted Antoinette's demeanor into Juliana, I would have had the perfect woman. Antoinette told me to keep her posted on my progress with Juliana. "It will be more entertaining than the telenovelas," she said, referring to the soap operas that are a Latin American cultural obsession.

Not that I didn't have the "right" to be with another girl, but as soon as Antoinette left I scoured my room for tell-tale signs—condom wrappers, lipstick-stained cigarette butts. Anything that might set Juliana off. The jasmine scent from Antoinette's perfume seemed to be ingrained in the sheets, so I tracked down the maid and urged her to change them. She didn't understand me; she could only see that I was frantic. She seemed to think I was accusing her of something, and started crying. So I called Orlando. Once again, he came through, calming down the maid and clarifying my request for fresh linens.

A little after eleven, Orlando called to tell me that Juliana had just phoned; she'd be at the hotel in about forty minutes. I was chewing my nails like termites feasting on a two by four. I only stopped when blood started dripping from my thumb. Every few minutes, I'd look out the window for Juliana.

The phone rang; I was sure it was her calling to cancel. Instead, it was Orlando: "She's on her way upstairs, Mister Joe."

I waited in the doorway. The damn elevators sucked in that hotel. Finally, one stopped and she stepped out.

Juliana didn't smile or speak as she approached me. But at the doorway, she playfully pushed me into the room and hugged me.

Then she said she loved me. I said it back to her without hesitation. I don't know which thrilled me more: her saying it to me, or me saying it to her. I hadn't been able to say it to anyone with conviction in a long time. I hadn't been in love with my last girlfriend, Karen. But once a relationship lingers, for whatever reasons, beyond a certain point, you feel obligated to say it. I'd never said it to Karen first, because that would have been too dishonest. But when she'd say it, I felt that I had to respond in kind.

With Juliana, though, there was truth in it. And it felt perfectly natural, exciting, to say it to her. I don't think either of us meant it unconditionally. She might have thought she loved me, in her impulsive way. And whatever I felt, I don't think it was the kind of love that forms a cornerstone for a life together. But as we held each other now, my hands pulsed—accompanied by bursts of percussion from the musicians outside practicing for Carnival—and I couldn't steady my fingers during foreplay. It was an intoxicating start.

Almost intoxicating enough to cause me to give in to her when she swiped the condom I was about to put on and demanded: "No condom. Give me a baby."

I froze for a minute while my mind searched for the appropriate response. It was insane—at least from my perspective—her wanting to get pregnant from someone she'd known less than a week. But I didn't want to be that blunt. The best thing was to try to convince her, without offending her, that it wasn't a practical idea.

"Someday. Not now," I said.

"Please."

I tried to tell her about my financial problems, that I didn't want to father a child that I wasn't sure I could help raise. My mother had raised me alone, and I knew the difficulties she'd faced. I was also concerned about sexual diseases, but they were almost an afterthought at that point.

"Please. Make a baby with me."

"We can't. Not yet."

"I don't like you," she said. She threw on her clothes, grabbed her shoes, and stormed out.

I wanted to run after her, but I was almost certain it wasn't necessary. Sure enough, Hurricane Juliana reversed course, knocking on my door a moment later. She greeted me with declarations of, "I love you; I love you." We made love; then I tried to lie back and digest everything that had happened since I got to Rio. Juliana lounged forward on the bed, absorbed in soap operas and cartoons. Still, she wanted to screw at nearly every commercial break, and would get a little petulant whenever I'd point to my genitals and say, *ainda dormindo*—still sleeping. I hadn't yet had the chance to take Antoinette's advice and buy "stud spinach" at the drugstore.

Later, as Juliana got ready to leave, I asked her what was an appropriate fee. Her response vanquished any doubts I still had about her interest in me. She refused to take any money, not even cab fare. All she wanted was $15 to cover what she'd be docked for missing a day at the brothel. I guess in Rio, even sex for money wasn't always straightforward.

On my last day in Rio, she took me to an amusement park where we got caught in a storm. Juliana was euphoric, dragging me all over the park (past restaurants and souvenir shops that would have made perfect shelters) until we found the haunted house. It was a lame ride, but we were out of the rain. Inside, Juliana grew even more ecstatic, screaming like a kid and pulling me close whenever we bumped into a cheap plastic skeleton or cardboard witch.

We wanted to spend the night together. First, we went to her house so she could change into dry clothes. When we got off the bus, we were ankle-deep in mud facing a dirt road lined with shacks. Two small riderless horses passed us at a lazy clip, as if they wanted to make sure we noticed them. I started laughing. "Why?" Juliana asked. Apparently this was a common sight in her neighborhood. I told her I'd never seen stray horses before. Stray dogs, yes. But stray horses? Never. At least not in Brooklyn.

We trudged through the mud for about ten minutes until we came to a grocery store that looked like a converted garage. I waited there while she went next door to her house. She returned with two surprises: her son and daughter. She had, of course, told me about them. But I didn't expect to meet them. Her kids were beautiful, and I started thinking how handsome their father must be. What the hell could Juliana possibly see in me? The girl, four, was shy and stayed close to Juliana. But the boy, a year younger, walked right up to me with a giant smile. I introduced myself in Portuguese, which must have been improving because he responded in kind, "*Eu sou Marco*"—I'm Marco.

Juliana had bad news, though. She couldn't go back with me to the hotel. It sounded like her mother wouldn't let her. Why, I wondered, would a twenty-five-year-old with two kids need her mother's permission? The mother came into the store and Juliana, looking upset, introduced us. She seemed pleasant, but the inherent awkwardness of meeting the mother of someone you initially paid for sex was made worse by the fact that unlike Juliana, who knew a few words of English (less than I'd thought, I was about to find out) the older woman didn't know any. After a few minutes of us pretending to understand each other, the mother took my arm and gestured for me to go with her.

I was getting nervous. "What's going on?" I asked Juliana. All I could make out was that her mother was taking me back to my hotel.

"Why?" I asked. "To have sex with me?"

Juliana burst into laughter.

It took a long time for Juliana to make me understand. Her mother would have watched the kids, but she had plans to meet friends downtown, not far from my hotel. Since I didn't know the way back, she was going to take the bus with me.

Clearly, my Portuguese was still a bit raw. Topping my to-do list for home: Take a damn Berlitz course. And thank my friend Ian, of course.

CHAPTER TWO

From Schmucking to Fucking

THE GIRLS ON IAN'S COMPUTER SCREEN MARKED A STRANGE contrast to the pungent cooking smells of borscht and pelmeni drifting through his apartment from his neighbors' kitchen. Ian, a middle-aged teacher from New York, had turned his screensaver into a virtual shrine to his many trips to Latin America. There was the sexy Brazilian Silvia on the beach in Rio de Janeiro; Ian and pretty redhead Gladys at a restaurant in Boca Chica in the Dominican Republic; Regina, another Brazilian, in his room in Rio licking her lips. Three dozen girls in all, continuously elbowing one another off the screen, each grabbing her five seconds in the spotlight.

Being Latina wasn't the only thing the women had in common: they were also all prostitutes. "I got the bug," Ian, my friend for nearly a decade, told me. "Mongering's an addiction."

Mongering. That's how growing ranks of men from developed nations refer to their travels abroad to pay for sex. Many mongers are as dedicated to sex tourism as serious skiers are to pilgrimages to the Alps. Ian had introduced me to the concept.

He didn't mind being called a monger, though I found it only slightly less sleazy than its root, *whoremonger*. Other possibilities were *whorist* and *hoe-ologist*, but they didn't enjoy much of a following among American sex tourists. *Sexpat* was good, but it was a play on *expatriate*, so it didn't encompass travelers. *Punter*, popular with Brits, also had a nice ring to it.

Ian seemed more comfortable with the monger label than I was, though my own overseas activities certainly qualified me.

Ian had met Silvia on one of his first trips to Rio, when she was in her early twenties. On each subsequent visit to Brazil, he spent time with the sandy-haired prostitute. Now he wanted to marry her and bring her to America. But the thought of settling down with— or settling for, in Ian's mind—a working girl tormented him. "Is that all I can get: a prostitute?" he'd ask. "Why can't I find a beautiful woman at home?" Ian (lacking a sense of irony) questioned Silvia's "moral fiber," wondering why one girl "flushes her morality down the toilet" by hooking while other girls from similar backgrounds choose different paths out of poverty. He also agonized over his own behavior, wondering why men like him would flush their own morality down the toilet by getting on a plane and going to these places.

He was obsessed with Silvia, but he couldn't "pull the trigger" and marry her. "There's too much baggage, divorce potential, and those fucking tattoos I hate," he reasoned charitably.

I tried to convince him that there was nothing wrong with marrying a prostitute. I would do it in a second, if and when I met the right one, I emailed him. "If Silvia and you really love each other, then you owe it to yourself to fully explore the idea of building a life with her. But this means that *before* getting married, you need to spend more time with her and find out certain things: What kind of life does she want for her children? Does she want them to go to college and be successful in a traditional profession? Does she understand that prostitution is viewed very differently in the United States than in Brazil? If you live here and have a daughter, will you and Silvia work hard to raise her with more traditional values?"

Ian worried about how Silvia would *behave* in America. "Find out exactly what she thinks about her profession," I told him. "Does she see it as a temporary part of her life that was mainly a way to make decent money? Or is she 'enamored' with that lifestyle? In other words, does she see herself as a perpetual 'party girl' who's always going to have a wild streak, whether or not she's getting paid to sleep with guys? Also, would Silvia be willing to accept the fact that her past must be kept secret? Is she willing to stick to a cover story that she was an office worker or a cashier in Brazil?"

Then there was the problem of religion—Ian was Jewish, Silvia, Catholic—though it seemed trivial compared to the issue of her trade. Ian was hardly religious, but he'd always imagined making his parents proud by bringing home a Jewish girl. (Silvia would eventually offer to convert, and even to laser off her tattoos, if it would make Ian happy.)

"Ultimately, I think it comes down to this," I said. "Can you be comfortable with your decision? Can you build a life with her and not be consumed by guilt? If the guilt will be too much, then you will be extremely unhappy. If guilt won't be a big factor, then you have more of a chance of experiencing real happiness with her."

Ian's friend Neil, a veteran monger from the States who's been to Rio countless times, was more cynical. He told Ian not to take a tiger out of its habitat. America was too different, he said—the weather, the people, prejudices, language. She might be unhappy. Plus, guys will be hitting on her all the time, he promised Ian. Guys with money.

"I know you like being with her," Neil said, "but usually marrying a prostitute spells disaster. If I met a girl today in Brazil that I really liked, and I was young, and my money was good, I'd knock her up, get her a good apartment, send money down there, go down as often as I could afford to, and retire there."

"No offense to Neil," I told Ian. "But this isn't about her coming here so she can enjoy the nightlife. It's also not about bringing her here so you can just keep fucking her. It's about you two making a life together, and this is the place to do it. New York may not be as much fun as Brazil, but we're hopefully talking about two people who want to settle down, and who don't have to go out every night to get their kicks. In fact, the whole reason you want her here is so that you can move onto the next phase of your life, where you don't need to bed different women (as great as that is, and I know, because I'm still stuck in that phase with no plans to leave it anytime soon) for fulfillment. And your career, which is financially rewarding, is here. If you decide to become a couple, then it makes sense that you'd put down roots in New York."

Neil acknowledged, however, that bringing Silvia to the States was worth a shot. "You'll never know if you don't try," he told Ian. "What's the worst that can happen? She'll get mad and go back to Brazil? Whether you marry a girl from here or there, it's going to be a gamble. If you like her enough, take the gamble. And if it doesn't work out, you know where to go to cure your blues. Remember the bright beaches of Rio."

I fully agreed. "If you got the balls," I told him, "then just fucking do it already. Otherwise, you'll hit the half-century mark and still be agonizing over Silvia."

Even after Silvia swore that she was leaving the sex trade, Ian had his doubts. A hard worker, she started a lunch counter on the ground floor of her house in a *favela*, one of Rio's hillside slums. But she treated Ian as her main source of funds, leaning on him for an oven and other high-ticket items. She also insisted he buy her things that had nothing to with business, like a car.

"I'm projecting that marrying you would be a mistake because I imagine that when I could not buy you the newest Mercedes or the biggest house, you would go with another man that was richer than me," Ian emailed her in English.

When he wasn't agonizing over Silvia, Ian was fun to be around. With his flair for foreign accents, he could have killed at an open-mike night. He was much better at keeping friends, male and female, than I was. He didn't mind being ribbed about his growing paunch and thinning hair. Those qualities might have made him more endearing to his friends, but his appearance limited his chances of finding a girlfriend in New York. As he'd gotten out of shape, he lost his appetite for the bar scene and Jewish singles parties.

Those days, Ian seemed to dwell, in Thoreau's chilling words from *Walden*, among "the mass of men lead[ing] lives of quiet desperation."

"F F F," he'd headlined an email in his typical cryptic style. Which stood for "Forty, Fat, Fucked."

"What is that?" I replied. "Title of a porn movie?" I knew he was miserable, but I couldn't resist the opportunity to tease him a bit, and hopefully make him laugh.

One time, he emailed this holiday greeting to friends: "Happy New Year??? Who will find a nice girl to marry? Or have a great gal who fucks like a goddess . . . ? Not me. . . . Who will face a tragedy? Who will lose his job . . . ? Who will keep the same crap job?"

"Very nice, very upbeat," I wrote back. "Makes me feel all warm and tingly inside."

I lent Ian my well-worn copy of *The Game: Penetrating the Secret Society of Pickup Artists, New York Times* reporter Neil Strauss's account of his journey through a subculture of "seduction gurus" and their followers who've adapted self-help psychology into an elaborate system for attracting girls. I also sent Ian a list of websites with detailed information on seduction techniques. I thought that learning how to meet women at home would boost his confidence.

Ian wasn't buying it. Rio makes it too easy to get laid, he said. And there was "no chance of rejection or wrong numbers."

"Apples and oranges," I said. "It's comparing a way of living life to the fullest during the 90 percent of the time we're at home, to that 10 percent (or less) that we're in 'Disney World.' They're totally different situations that require different approaches for maximum benefit."

Of course, the more I tried to master these seduction techniques myself, the more I realized how much dedication they required. They weren't meant for a lazy, undisciplined fuck like me, who thrived on the theory that the best things in life, if not free, shouldn't require much effort. Eventually, it would become clear that Rio was made as much for me as it was for Ian.

Ian's escapades abroad had only made the singles scene at home less appealing for him. Even when he ventured out on a date, he usually found cause for complaint. "I'm so jaded now from Rio," he emailed me before a blind date. "It's totally warped my mindset of how women can and should be." Ian had already decided that his date would suck.

Of course, he still had Silvia. But that relationship was hardly ideal. Still, Ian's quandary regarding Silvia was the kind of problem he might have yearned for eight years earlier when he found himself alone in his cramped living room on yet another Saturday night. He'd read something that week calling Rio's Carnival a public orgy. All you have to do is show up, the article promised. If it were true, he thought, Carnival might make up for all those times at Club Med where he'd met plenty of women but never experienced a single moment of romance. So he fixated on Rio and Carnival and sex until it propelled him off of his couch and over to his computer. He searched the Internet, and at the top of the results he found something called the World Sex Guide (WSG).

Not knowing anything about the World Sex Guide or mongering, he innocently dove into the website's reports on Carnival. The first few posts said little about the festival itself, and mainly warned mongers not to give in to the inflated prices that Brazilian prostitutes charged during Carnival. That information was irrelevant to Ian, who had no interest in hookers at the time.

The next post started off with promise, though, praising Carnival as a sex spectacle where "regular" Brazilian girls loved to party with gringos. But it ended with the caveat that the guys have to be "young, cute, and speak a little Portuguese." It didn't exactly leave Ian hopeful about his chances of scoring with Brazilian girls. Another report, however, perked him up, advising Americans to avoid prostitutes and "find some regular girls . . . Everybody will be drunk and high so you will be getting laid regardless." But then came the kicker: "This doesn't apply to you if you are a sixty-five-year-old, 400-pound whale."

To Ian, it might as well have read "lonely, middle-aged, overweight loser." If he wanted to get rejected, he reasoned, he could always just go to a bar in Manhattan. But out of curiosity, he scanned the World Sex Guide's reports on Brazilian hookers. Many of the posts described a staple of monger culture, the *GFE*, the "Girlfriend Experience," which seemed to blur the lines between paid sex and real intimacy.

"Bwana Dik," for example, who posted yearly guides to "the good life in Rio," wrote about Sabrina, "a petite, dark-haired beauty." She worked at a terma—hybrids of upscale strip clubs, health spas, and whorehouses that are as much of an institution in Rio as the *rodizio* restaurants serving traditional Brazilian barbecue. As Bwana Dik sat at the bar, Sabrina's dancing completely mesmerized him. She noticed him watching her dance, winked, came over and they exchanged kisses. He pointed out that in a terma, you can sit out in the bar area and talk, kiss, and fondle at great length, which the girls in these establishments really seem to enjoy. Bwana Dik's account helped shift Ian's attitude on prostitution. It also foreshadowed my own first GFE in Rio some years later.

Ian kept at it till morning, digesting dozens of posts about Brazil and the Dominican Republic.

His experience shows how sites like the World Sex Guide and its main rival, the International Sex Guide, have helped catapult sex tourism into the global age, providing an ever-expanding clearinghouse for everything from finding the cheapest brothels to preventing dehydration on long flights by avoiding alcohol. By 2008, the World Sex Guide claimed more than 215,000 members and 413,000 posts while the International Sex Guide claimed more than 211,000 members and 546,000 posts.

"Unless your father's a sailor," said Ian, "how would you get the details on what these places are really like? The official tourism boards aren't going to promote it."

As the Internet brings sex tourism more into the mainstream, the potential number of mongers becomes enormous. According to the 2000 census, 21 million men age twenty-five to fifty-four were either separated from their spouses, divorced, or never married; 11 million men were living alone. A 2004 study from the National Marriage Project of Rutgers University found the lifetime probability of divorce or separation close to 50 percent for the average couple marrying in recent years.

Another study, *ABC News*'s 2004 "American Sex Survey," demolishes the notion that singles are swinging, claiming that even among young singles (under thirty), nearly half aren't dating at all. Here's an even clearer hint to mongering's potential: The survey found that 15 percent of all males and 30 percent of single men age thirty and older have paid for sex.

Loneliness itself seems to be on the rise. A report from the June 2006 American Sociological Review found that Americans' circle of confidants has closed in on itself from a mean of 2.94 in 1985 to 2.08 in 2004. The report also said the number of people who felt they had nobody to discuss important matters with more than doubled in that span, to nearly 25 percent.

All of these studies suggest a significant number of men are longing for physical and emotional intimacy. Of course, some of those statistics include women, too, which may help explain why female sex tourism is also on the rise. Still, women have never flocked to prostitutes in the numbers that men have.

* * * *

As globalization's digital nervous system, the Internet seemed predestined to become an engine to drive sex tourism. Demand for online porn helped spark the Internet's emergence as a mass medium in the 1990s; consumers of vicarious sex meant prospects for the real thing, and online ads for prostitutes soon followed. The University of Rhode Island's Donna Hughes, an expert on the sex trade, accords Seattle's A Personal Touch Services the dubious honor of being the first escort service to launch a website. The Internet Business Journal said the site was 1994's most significant online marketing innovation. By 1995, a website for an operation called Pimps 'R' Us was pitching sex trips to Nevada and the Dominican Republic. The tours included a guide who would provide "practical information about how to find and deal with prostitutes and how to arrange group orgies." Seizing on the opportunity, other websites for sex travel to Asia, Europe, Latin America, and the Caribbean quickly began popping up.

Meantime, sex tourists began posting accounts of their overseas encounters to the newsgroup alt.sex.prostitution. The World Sex Guide built a membership by archiving the reports and organizing them geographically. The site promoted itself as "comprehensive, sex-related information about every country in the world." Its first slogan was, "Fuckers of the world unite!" followed by, "Where do you want to fuck today?" In 1998, it tried to mellow its image, calling itself, "A research project about prostitution worldwide."

WSG proved to be an invaluable research tool for Ian. Shortly after his all-night cram session, Ian traveled to Boca Chica, a gritty seaside sex haven near the Dominican capital, Santo Domingo. It was the first of many visits to Latin America for Ian, who today spends about $20,000 a year on five or six trips to Rio and Boca Chica. He's been robbed at knifepoint twice in Rio, but the incidents haven't inhibited his wanderlust. "I'm miserable in New York," he says. "I'm always staring at the calendar, counting the days till my next trip, so I can go from schmucking"—Ian-speak for languishing at home—"to fucking."

A few nights before one of his Brazilian outings in 2008, he indulged his flair for the dramatic in an email to me:

"It's 1:17 a.m. and Ian is up late. . . . He is thinking of his trip to Rio and his lonely life in New York City. He will have fun in the Disney World of man's dreams. He will travel far, spend a week, then have to come home to the same old song and dance. He will go back to his job and be like everyone else except he will be much sadder because his gals and one gal in particular are not around."

A few days later, he wrote, "Joe, I feel like a sleazeball. I'm ashamed of my behavior in Rio. Though great fun. But I feel low. I was not raised like this."

My reply: "So give me your ticket. I'll go in your place. I have no worries about feeling like a sleazeball."

Once he got to Brazil, though, Ian's mood changed, as it always did there. "I'm so fucking addicted to this place," he emailed from Rio. He'd be joining Silvia in another part of the country in a few days. "But Ana licked my ass and sucked my dick so good I don't want to leave."

Shortly after he came home, he sent me two photos that summed up the Rio experience. The first captured movie star Bruce Willis with a hot brunette, the other showed a similar-looking girl that Ian had fucked in Brazil.

Still, these trips were and are no cure-all. "What if we're fifty and still doing this?" he often asks.

My answer is that if we're still going overseas and banging gorgeous women at fifty, we'll be heroes to guys half our age and to married guys who can only dream of that kind of thing. They'll treat us like Hugh Hefner. For me, if I meet the right girl, then great! If I'm still single but able to continue having sexcapades overseas . . . well, that's great too.

I know this is cold comfort to Ian, whose ultimate fantasy seems to be finding a soul mate and settling down. I'm in better shape than Ian, and not as burnt out on the singles scene, so I usually have an easier time than him meeting regular women at home. But Ian's life is much more settled at this point. He's got a steady teaching job, a growing nest egg, and a nice apartment with plenty of room for a girlfriend or wife. He's got a lot more to offer a potential spouse than I do these days. My writing assignments are unsteady, I owe a small fortune to the credit card companies, and I live in a rundown apartment. (True, the place could be magnificent if I had the will to fix the peeling paint, replace the ratty carpet, change the discolored linoleum in the kitchen, and buy some new living-room furniture.)

If Ian overcomes his angst and marries Silvia, he'll trade up from a GFE to what I call the PWE, the *Pretty Woman* Experience. I doubt that many men go abroad to find a wife among prostitutes. But as I've told Ian, such a fairytale romance would not only allow him to marry a girl he loves, but to rescue her from a life of poverty in a community where drug gangs hold sway. Does that mean Ian and Silvia would live happily ever after in America? Maybe, maybe not. They'd get the same guarantee of lifelong bliss that every other couple gets.

Sex tourists as a whole probably aren't a bad lot; many just want consensual sex with women of legal age. The World Sex Guide seems justified in describing its membership as a "community of men (and some women) who enjoy sexual relationships with other consenting adults."

But like consumers who buy the fruits of sweatshop labor, mongers also help to fuel, intentionally or not, the darker aspects of the international sex trade. As globalization has made borders more porous, the demand for prostitutes has grown. Much of it is met through trafficking in young men and women, including large numbers of children, who wind up in the sex trade through force or false promises of "honest work" abroad. A U.S. government report estimates that 600,000 to 800,000 people are trafficked across international borders each year, most of whom end up in the sex trade. About 80 percent of those trafficked are female, and up to 50 percent are minors. The report cautions that its focus is international trafficking, so the numbers don't include the "millions of victims who are trafficked within their own national borders."

In a three-part series on sex tourism for *GQ*, writer Sean Flynn noted that UNICEF estimates trafficking victims at between 700,000 and 2,000,000, "also mostly women and also mostly in the sex trade, which [UNICEF] says is the third-most-lucrative black-market business on the planet, behind only weapons and drugs." As Flynn wrote, "The International Labor Organization calculates worldwide profits from sex trafficking at $27.8 billion a year, and the Federal Bureau of Investigation says the transnational trade (moving people from one country to another) is worth $9.5 billion." But he included a caveat that all those figures are "impossible to verify." Estimates of prostitutes by country, city, or "even specific red-light districts vary wildly, from lowball official figures to the incredibly overstated numbers conjured by aid groups and activists. Thailand, for instance, has either 75,000 prostitutes, as the government claims, or depending on which aid group is tossing out numbers, nearly two million who generate up to fourteen percent of the country's gross domestic product."

Brazil, the land of Ian's (and my own) dreams, is a huge player in the global sex trade. Advocacy group the Protection Project says that in 2000 as many as 75,000 women from Brazil had been smuggled into European countries using Portugal as an entry point—a huge operation involving up to one hundred organized gangs. Brazil, along with Thailand and the Philippines, is one of the top three countries in the world when it comes to the number of women working overseas in the sex trade, apparently. The group notes that two women rescued from a Portuguese brothel in 2001 implicated several Rio de Janeiro police officers in a trafficking ring. Brazilian authorities believed that the operation mainly targeted minors and was linked to organized crime in Spain and Portugal.

Time magazine ran a somewhat amusing story on Brazilian prostitutes in the Portuguese town of Bragança. The piece hinted, however, that "clean" but complacent government bureaucrats may unwittingly be useful to traffickers. About three hundred Brazilian prostitutes have set up shop in Bragança. They've infuriated the local wives, who've accused them of drugging and even bewitching their husbands with black magic. Some of the wives started a petition drive to oust the Brazilians. They took the petition to the police chief, António Magalhaes de Oliveira. "In Portugal, there is no such thing as prostitution," he told *Time.* "It's the wives' problems to solve with their husbands, not the problem of police. The wives," he said, "better start making themselves more interesting to their husbands!"

CHAPTER THREE

Erotic City

D*ID THEY POISON ME?* PETER WONDERED AS HE GREW WEAKER. Should he have known better than to take a drink from these girls? Through his window, he could still hear the crowd milling about outside Help Discoteca. He could even make out the waves—but barely—breaking on Copacabana Beach.

The girls lay on either side of him. The white girl was whispering in Portuguese: "*Helasha*, baby." Relax. He tried to tell her to go fuck herself. But the words just floated in his head, garbled. Peter could feel the black girl with the ferocious blue eyes kissing his neck. Fucking bloodsucker. He wanted to shove her away, but his limbs no longer responded to his will.

There had been nothing odd in the way the vodka had tasted that night. The odd thing was how insistent the girls had been that he finish it. When he protested that he'd had enough, when he tried to explain about drinking and his libido and "diminishing returns," the girls reignited him by pouring the vodka all over each other. It turned him on, but it was fear of seeming timid that made him lick it off.

But such concerns were trivial compared to what he feared now, as he tried to stay conscious. Had he spun the wheel one too many times? Was it cosmic payback for being a role model at home—as a drug counselor in Los Angeles, he tried to steer kids away from prostitution—and a "player" here? He could visualize a headline: "Youth Counselor Dead After Night with Hookers in Rio."

Peter's first visit to Rio seven years before had started out draped in idealism, as a quest for a soul mate. He'd wanted to find someone like Antonia, his cousin Ron's Brazilian wife. Antonia had luminous hazel eyes that locked on you and glowed at even the most mundane comment. It wasn't so much that you wanted to grab her and take her on the spot, Ron be damned—of course you did—it was that every gaze from Antonia, every syllable in her teasing tropical accent suggested that she wanted to tear into *you*. Three years into the marriage, Ron still seemed entranced with Antonia. "Just give me her fingernail so I can clone her," Peter would tell Ron.

"Seriously, go to Rio," Ron urged. He prepped Peter for his wife-hunt by recommending upscale beaches and nightclubs. "But learn some Portuguese before you go." Peter, always overextended, felt there was no time. He reasoned that he could pick it up bit by bit in Rio, but he was wrong. Peter could move well enough to break the ice on the dance floor, but off the floor affluent Brasileiras had little patience for gringos with limited Portuguese.

Having grown tired of ending every night in a tropical paradise alone, he remembered something Ron had told him before he left for Rio, about the hookers at Help. "Forget about finding a wife in there," Ron said. "But you can't go to Rio without going to Help at least once." So Peter went to Help once, which turned into twice, which turned into three times, four times, until it became his nightly ritual.

Help, opposite the beach on Copacabana's main drag, Avenida Atlantica, is something of a racial utopia, at least for mongers. (Brazil's one hell of a melting pot, a genetic smorgasbord formed over centuries from the region's indigenous tribes, Portuguese conquerors, African slaves, and later waves of Italians, Germans, and others.) A typical crowd includes mocha-skinned girls with blue eyes, blondes with sharp Italian features, and Amazonian Indians with long jet-black hair. It was outside Help that the black girl with ferocious blue eyes had approached Peter about a threesome.

Help's name is a tribute to The Beatles, whose engravings line the staircase from the coat check up to the dance floor. Help opened in the early 1980s as just another Copacabana nightclub. According to "Bravo," a contributor to the International Sex Guide, rumor has it that Help initially didn't allow prostitutes. But a lawsuit changed all that, claiming that sex workers who paid the entrance fees had just as much right to enter as anyone. Prostitutes scored a victory in court, and thus began the transformation of Help from a regular nightspot into a magnet for working girls and sex tourists.

The travel experts at Frommer's take a tougher line on Help's history: "When this disco opened at the height of the early eighties craze, its dazzling lightshow and monster dance floor drew the young and beautiful by the beachload. It was the place to be seen. Two decades later, the unrefurbished Help attracts only lonely gringo travelers and Brazilian working girls; no self-respecting

Carioca woman would be seen in the place, which means that beautiful dark-eyed lovely with whom you're getting on so well is most definitely expecting payment."

Today, after seven years and countless visits to Help, the very system Peter had mastered as a veteran traveler to Rio enabled the two girls in his room to get away with whatever it was they had in mind. In his early mongering days, Peter had learned that Rio's hotels—at least the reputable ones—had strict policies on prostitutes. For a surcharge, you could bring one girl back to your room. But two? Out of the question. And she had to be gone by morning, sometimes as early as five. Otherwise you'd get an unscheduled wake-up call or knock on the door to remind you.

True mongers didn't stay at hotels. They rented apartments in the old buildings that lined the side streets of Copacabana. For fifty dollars a night, you could get a decent-sized room in a gated building with a doorman. Who you took upstairs was your business. But hotels provided a crucial layer of security that apartments didn't. The front desk would check a girl's ID to make sure she wasn't a minor. Then they'd hold it till she left, calling you first to make sure everything was all right. Peter's doorman provided no such service. As long as the girls didn't try to leave with a sofa or stove, he'd buzz them out the gate without much fuss.

It couldn't have been more than a few minutes since the girls had given him what he'd paid for. In fact, he'd paid about half the going rate for a threesome in Copacabana. The girls' willingness to accept a lower fee had been a red flag, but he'd chalked it up to luck and charisma. True, he'd been wary that he'd never seen them before. Not at Help, where they'd approached him, nor in any of his favorite brothels. But that had been part of their appeal. It wasn't always easy finding fresh faces in the same old places.

Peter had been to Brazil enough times to joke that he was an *Amerioca*, a play on the word for a native of Rio, *Carioca*. He'd heard of all the stories, scams, and set-ups of gringos by teams of prostitutes and police. But he'd never experienced this. A recent murder, allegedly by a prostitute, of a Russian in town for a technology conference had given him pause. But not enough to keep him away. Copacabana, of course, had plenty of muggings, even in daylight, but he'd been spared those, too. Maybe growing up in South Central Los Angeles caused him to give off a vibe that told predators they'd have an easier time with someone else. The worst that had happened to him in Rio was the shit-on-the-shoes bit: as you're walking near the beach, a kid smears feces on your footwear and vanishes before you know what happened; then his baby-faced young associate races up with a shoe-shine box, points to the crap and offers to buff it out of existence.

Tonight more than his shoes were at stake.

With Peter's consciousness fading, the two girls in his bed were a dissipating blur of vanilla perfume and whispers and hair brushing against his mouth. He could still recall negotiating with them earlier that night, and how willing they were to accept a ridiculously low price. The idea of a threesome was always appealing, but he'd had plenty of them since he started coming to Brazil; and he wasn't a thirteen-year-old anymore, choking on his own testosterone, when passing up any chance at sex was tantamount to self-asphyxiation. Hence he'd held out until they accepted his offer of . . . how much was it? Various numbers danced in his mind until his mind went dark.

But luckily for Peter there'd be no headlines in the American newspapers about a youth counselor murdered by Brazilian prostitutes. It was the first thing Peter realized as he came to in the morning. The girls were gone. The bedroom was in shambles; they'd combed through his stuff looking for valuables. But all they'd taken was his portable DVD player. The only other signs of disruption were the dirty dishes and empty food packages strewn around the tiny kitchenette. The girls must have worked up an appetite, and they helped themselves to steak and eggs. Clearly, they hadn't been in a rush, so they must have had a good idea how long the drug would last.

Good thing their talents for thievery didn't match their pharmaceutical skills. Peter's money and passport remained untouched in the locked hall closet. He found the key still stuffed in its hiding place, a balled-up pair of socks that the girls had apparently flung across the room as just more crap of little interest.

Peter's been back to Rio several times since. Like Ian, he accepts the risks.

He never reported the incident to the police. "I'd have to be insane," he tells me over drinks at Terraco Atlantico, the sidewalk café next door to Help. "It would mean putting myself on record as an American who fucks hookers. That's not illegal, but if the wrong cop sees it, maybe I get blackmailed. Besides, they're never going to investigate a robbery over a bullshit DVD player."

"What about the girls? Ever see them again?"

"Never. I think they're too smart to show up at Help too often."

Peter explains that a minimal level of trust has to exist for the sex trade in Copacabana to flourish.

"Everybody knows each other here—the garotas, the regular mongers. Even if girls like the ones that robbed me don't get in trouble with the police, their reputations will still be fucked and every guy will avoid them like they had AIDS."

He asks if I think the robbery was "karma."

"How so?" I ask.

"You know. My job's keeping kids away from this life. Yet here I am fucking anything that moves."

* * * *

As one of Latin America's most violent cities, with murders exceeding 60 per 100,000 people, Rio is full of risks. So is Brazil overall. A typical flight from New York to Rio requires changing planes in Brazil's largest city, São Paulo. When I went to Brazil in May of 2006, São Paulo was in the midst of a series of deadly attacks orchestrated by the "First Capital Command," a gang whose tentacles had grown far beyond its spawning ground in the local prisons. Meanwhile, I was on a plane at São Paulo's Guarulhos International Airport for the short flight to Rio. We sat on the tarmac without explanation for the delay, so I asked a flight attendant. She said we were waiting for passengers on a late connecting flight from France because the airline didn't want them to have to stay in the city overnight. It had the aura of the fall of Saigon.

If São Paulo is Saigon, then Rio sometimes evokes Pompeii in its final days. At the end of 2006, gangs attacked police and civilians in Rio, killing at least nineteen, including eight victims of a bus torching. Authorities said it was a show of force to get the attention of Rio State's incoming governor. The attacks also might have been reprisals for challenges to drug gangs' control of *favelas*, the hillside shantytowns where more than a million Cariocas live, from militias of off-duty and former police.

Dangerous or not, Brazil remains a magnet for sex tourists. It's worth the risks. Walk around Rio's mongering heart, Copacabana, any night (albeit carefully) from late September through June—Brazilian spring and summer—and you'll see the cafés and bars teeming with Americans, Canadians, Italians, and Germans flirting with the working girls. Prostitution is legal in Brazil. Pimping isn't, and the absence—at least on the surface—of feral middlemen in Copacabana is one of the things that makes this fabled beach community so appealing to sex tourists. There's no doubt that pimps are involved in the sex trade there, but of all the countless hours I've spent in Copacabana, I've only noticed local men a few times hanging around the garotas. Also, many of the girls make a point of their independence. These, of course, are unreliable yardsticks; some of the girls have to have "boyfriends" waiting at home for their share of the profits.

Prostitution is embedded in the culture in ways that might surprise some Americans. The Brazilian government's directory of occupations advises those who wish to make a living as a "sex professional" (it rates its own category, 5198) to, "Seduce with your glance . . . charm with your voice . . . conquer with your touch." Along with sexually transmitted diseases and violence, the directory lists "inhalation of vehicle fumes" as an occupational risk.

Category 5198 originally included *fazer companhia ao turista*—providing company for a tourist—among a prostitute's tasks. But the tourism minister learned of the reference and complained that it contradicted Brazil's official stance against sex travel. The bureaucrats in charge of the directory quickly deleted it. They claimed that their intention never was to promote sex tourism, and that the overall purpose of Category 5198 was to help health officials plan educational campaigns. They also said they weren't making any value judgments about prostitution by including it in the directory. Damage control or not, official recognition of prostitution enhances Brazil's reputation as a haven for carnal commerce.

One of the government's health campaigns created a new pop-culture icon, a busty cartoon hooker named "Maria Without Shame." Health officials teamed with prostitutes to blanket the country with pamphlets featuring Maria urging her fellow sex workers to use condoms and to "Value your work. Don't be ashamed, girl. You're a professional." Although such colorful efforts might add to the mixed signals about Brazil's erotic image, they've also contributed to the relatively low, stable rate of HIV infection among its female sex workers—about 6 percent in 2005.

The exuberance of "Maria Without Shame" had a counterpoint in Rio de Janeiro State's ham-fisted attempt a few years back to reduce the area's sex appeal by restricting postcards of bikini-clad Brasileiras. How much impact can that have in an age when a place's image is increasingly shaped by word of mouse at websites like the World Sex Guide?

The Internet's even given new life to "Carnival in Rio," a racy 1983 travel video in which a pre-*Terminator*, on-the-brink-ofmega-stardom Arnold Schwarzenegger lavishes attention on samba dancers' most celebrated anatomical asset.

Another video shot in Rio, Snoop Dogg's 2003 "Beautiful," showcased stunning Cariocas on the beach. "Beautiful" reportedly drew a new wave of sex tourists to Rio. Spelman College history professor William Jelani Cobb discussed the link in a controversial article in *Essence*. He noted a surge in African-American visitors to Brazil in recent years. "By most accounts, sex tourism is driving this increase," he wrote, adding that "many locals believe the latest outbreak of Rio fever is inspired at least in part by hip-hop's glamorization of the city."

Brazilians who want to tone down the country's image are up against more than rap videos. They also face the growing political clout of Brazil's prostitutes. Sex workers won a symbolic, but notable, victory in 2005 when Brazil rejected 40 million dollars in U.S. funding to help fight AIDS. The rejection was in protest of the Bush administration's requirement that recipients—in this case, partnerships with prostitutes, like the coalition behind the "Maria Without Shame" campaign—condemn prostitution.

Working girls also proved their lobbying prowess when the Association of Prostitutes of Bahia won permission to start an FM station, Radio Zona, in the city of Salvador. The group's spokesman told Reuters that Zona wouldn't focus on recruiting new prostitutes. But neither would it "apologize for prostitution." It would "struggle for the dignity of the profession." The line-up would include programs about AIDS prevention and human rights.

Davida, a Rio-based prostitute advocacy group, had a more immediate impact on Brazil's popular culture with the launch of its own clothing line, "Daspu," a name that's both an abbreviation of *das putas* ("from the prostitutes") and a gibe at Brazilian fashion emporium Daslu. Daspu has generated loads of coverage, including a piece in the Brazilian edition of *Vogue* that featured the clothing line's prostitute models.

Daspu, though, has hardly been a blip on the media's radar compared to Raquel Pacheco, aka Bruna "Surfer Girl" Surfistinha. She catapulted to fame through online accounts of her life as a high-priced escort in São Paulo. According to the *New York Times*, it was the most popular blog in Brazil. Her steamy anecdotes set off a national debate about sexual values, leading to a publishing deal and a best-selling memoir, *O Doce Veneno do Escorpião* (*The Scorpion's Sweet Venom*). An American edition was published in 2007, and a film adaptation is in the works.

Brazil's 2000 census counted 125 million Catholics, roughly 73 percent of the population, down from 92 percent in 1970. Even with that drop, Brazil remains the largest Catholic nation on earth, a strange setting for glorification of prostitutes. But the numbers disguise the essence of Brazil's brand of Catholicism. Anthropologist Richard Parker notes that the country's Portuguese settlers brought with them the sensual character of Portugal's Catholic tradition: "its festivals and village feasts in honor of the saints who . . . offered assistance in matters of love . . . its remarkably relaxed sexual morality." Parker says modern Brazilians see this "as a key source for the unusual degree of sensuality that marks Brazilian life even today."

In Rio, you'll find brothels in shopping malls, across the street from churches, and next door to banks. As you weave through the throngs of shoppers, for instance, at Siqueira Campos by Copacabana's main train station, it's impossible to miss the garish sign for "L'Uomo," a whorehouse on the top level of an open-air mall.

It's not just big cities in Brazil where you find this openness. The northeastern town of Espertantina recently created an annual Orgasm Day. The mayor hopes the holiday, which includes panel discussions on premature ejaculation and other sexual subjects, will improve the relationships of married couples.

The paradox of Brazil's Catholicism might best be symbolized by the huge statue of Christ the Redeemer overlooking Rio from the peak of the 2,296-foot Corcovado mountain, his outstretched arms seeming to welcome everyone to the city, even sex tourists. If the statue could really make his feelings known about the debauchery below, I suspect his eyes would well up like "Iron Eyes Cody," the crying Native American in the old "Keep America Beautiful" commercial.

This would stand in marked contrast to Brazil's native populations, who apparently only knew tears of joy during their first encounters with Europeans in the early sixteenth century. The indigenous tribes that welcomed the young Portuguese sailors to South America's Atlantic coast were, according to historians' accounts, just as horny as their sea-weary guests. "No sooner had the European leaped ashore than he found his feet slipping among the naked Indian women," wrote Brazilian sociologist Gilberto Freyre. "They would give themselves to the European for a comb or a broken mirror."

Pero Vaz de Caminha, who accompanied explorer Pedro Alvares Cabral in 1500 on his discovery of Brazil, told Portugal's king, "One of those maidens was completely dyed, both below and above her waist, and surely was so well made up and so round, and her shameful part (that had no shame) so gracious, that many women from our land, seeing her countenance, will feel shame in not having theirs like hers."

As accounts like these drifted back to Europe, more sailors came, making Brazil a nation essentially founded on sex tourism. Official policy seemed to favor this libidinous activity as it allowed Portugal, with its relatively small population, to stay competitive with Spanish Conquistadors by creating generations of mixed blood particularly well-suited to colonizing the New World.

By the mid-1500s, Brazil was involved in the slave trade, ultimately importing almost 40 percent of the 11 million souls transported to the New World, making Brazil the Americas' biggest exploiter of African slaves. This was hardly a recipe for a racial paradise, but Africans became integral to Brazil's dynamic mix. The emerging nation's "sexual hyperesthesia," wrote Brazilian essayist Paulo Prado, "avoided the segregation of the African element that occurred in the United States. . . . Here lust and social laxity . . . united the races. . . . The seduction of the Portuguese settler by the *negra* and the *mulata* would become legendary."

Prado's take, published in 1928, still provokes intense debate in modern Brazil, where the huge gap between rich and poor closely follows racial lines. Yet most Brazilians defy racial categories. Around half of the country's 180 million people have African ancestors, but only 6.2 percent consider themselves black.

But while racial tension in Brazil is a problem, it is not as alarming as the rampant epidemic of underage prostitution. UNICEF says that there are about 500,000 underage prostitutes in Brazil. A 2005 study from the Brazilian government found child prostitution rings operating in nearly a thousand cities, including Rio and São Paulo. The statistics can be debated, but anecdotal evidence also paints a chilling picture of sexual exploitation in Brazil. Police in Italy helped to reveal where some of the demand comes from, busting a group of "travel agents" in 2004 for arranging annual outings to Brazil for a thousand men seeking sex with minors.

Why Brazil? As a United Nations report on child prostitution put it: "The touristic image of Brazil is all too often associated with stereotypical representations of young women, mainly Afro-Brazilians, portrayed half naked in tourist catalogues to convey the message that exotic sexual adventures can easily be available to tourists during their stay in the country."

Poverty is also a key factor driving child prostitution in Brazil. As Latin America's largest economy and the world's ninth largest, Brazil had a GDP of close to $800 billion in 2005. But it also has the tenth most unequal distribution of income. Brazil's wealthiest 50 percent earn nearly 90 percent of the total income. The government estimates that 40 million people live in extreme poverty.

The average monthly wage in Brazil's six largest cities was about $330 in November 2004. But a typical prostitute in Copacabana can easily pull in $70–$100 a night.

As part of Brazil's efforts against child prostitution, the justice ministry has been tracking statistics on sex crimes involving children. Brazil has also broadened the legal definition of trafficking to cover victims of both sexes, and equalized the penalties for domestic and international sex trafficking. Trafficking in young victims now carries a stiffer prison term. The U.S. State Department has commended Brazil on these moves.

UNICEF has been helping Brazilian police to recognize the forged identity cards that many underage prostitutes use. And in the last few years, Brazil has been running campaigns during Carnival to remind tourists that sex with minors can get them four to ten years in prison. The warnings are posted at airports and popular tourist spots. In Rio, tourism officials distribute guidelines to hotels, nightclubs, restaurants, taxi companies, and tourist agencies threatening them with loss of their licenses if they show visitors where to find underage prostitutes. The guidelines also call on them to report suspicious activities. But it's an uphill fight. Asked by the *San Francisco Chronicle*, about a dozen hotel employees in Copacabana said "they would not report tourists with an underage prostitute for fear of losing their jobs."

As previously mentioned, the Brazilian government has partnered with sex workers to score impressive victories against HIV. Yet not everyone in Rio seems to have gotten Maria Without Shame's safe-sex message. Mongers cheerfully post online about finding garotas who have no problem giving "BBBJs" (bareback blow jobs). Then there's the recklessness of gringos and garotas in the heat of the moment. On the World Sex Guide, "Bigdicki" writes about a working girl who tried to mount him without a condom. When he resisted, she ended the session and demanded her money. He paid her and sent her the hell out.

I'm glad that my own little condom caper with Juliana didn't end the same way.

CHAPTER FOUR

She-Devils, Bad; Lesbians, Good

Not only did I take a Berlitz course in basic Portuguese when I returned stateside, I also got translation software, started reading Brazilian newspapers online, and wrote emails to Brazilians I'd met, agonizing over every word to make my translations as accurate as possible. To impress Juliana, I needed to speak her language. I'd never been so zealous about learning.

I also developed a renewed interest in freelance writing. Except now it wasn't politics or keeping felons off the streets that got my juices flowing. My goal was to nab an assignment on Rio's sex culture that would allow me to defray the cost of my next trip. It would be a dream assignment, essentially getting paid to get laid. An editor's blessing would also allow me to feel better about going off to engage in more mongering, as I'd be able to offset my carnal activities with a higher journalistic purpose.

Hustler liked my idea for an article, and I returned to Rio in August 2003. And as luck would have it, I'd also obtained a more virtuous assignment from a law-enforcement magazine to cover a criminology conference in town. Of the two magazines, *Hustler* paid a lot more, and I quickly learned that when it comes to earning money as a freelancer, vice beats virtue every time. I really needed to give serious thought to writing more for porn magazines, I noted to myself.

On my first day back in Brazil, I made a surprise visit to see Juliana at Quatro por Quatro. She seemed happy to see me, but she spent most of the afternoon dwelling on her financial troubles. If I'd had enough money to solve her problems, I would have done so without hesitation, but I was nearly broke myself. Juliana was a big part of the reason I'd returned to Rio. I'd anticipated stepping effortlessly back into the romantic fantasy she'd helped me to build. That fantasy centered on both of us constantly glowing in each other's company, ravenous for each other day and night. But unlike the fantasy, the sex between us that afternoon was passionless. Afterward, I couldn't justify spending a big chunk of my trip with her only to have my fantasy come apart. So I decided it was better to make a clean break and seek my fantasies elsewhere. I didn't call or drop in anymore; she didn't contact me either.

I might have made more of an effort to keep things on track with Juliana, but I was also preoccupied with getting photos for my *Hustler* article. Without good pictures, the editor had stressed, the story would never run and all I'd get paid was a 25 percent kill fee. I didn't need anything fancy, just photos that would illustrate some of Rio's sex appeal.

Rio had plenty of photogenic working girls. The problem was that many of them didn't want to appear as representatives of their profession in an international magazine. In the end I had to approach dozens of girls before I found any willing to be photographed.

I saw a mocha-skinned prospect sitting in the window at Meia Pataca, the café on the next block from Help. Daniela had jet-black hair and looked like she appeared out of the mists of the Amazon rainforest. Pocahontas with lip gloss. I joined her for a drink. Innocent chitchat gave way to something else. "So, you like my tits?" she asked, pushing her breasts together. They were huge and I liked them very much. I tried not to stare, but she yanked my head to her chest. I must have looked quite ridiculous, but I was hooked. I only needed a few hours to do the photo shoot (or my point-and-click amateur version of one), but there was no way I'd be satisfied only taking pictures of her, and I didn't want her for just an hour or two. Instead I wanted to wear myself out fucking her, fall asleep on her amazing tits, and then bang her again at the crack of dawn.

We negotiated a deal for sex and photos. I think we settled on $150 for a whole night together. My hotel forbade visitors after 5 a.m., so I suggested VIPs, a motel in nearby Leblon that didn't bother with such restrictions. Daniela insisted on her apartment. I could have understood if a more timid prostitute had feared leaving Copacabana with a stranger. But Daniela? She had a dangerous air about her, and I was the one concerned about letting her pick the place. After we argued a bit, I told her the deal was off. There were plenty of garotas around, I reminded her, who wouldn't give me a hard time. Reluctantly, she agreed to go to VIPs.

But first we went to my hotel so I could grab a few things. I would have had to pay a guest fee to bring her to my room, so I asked her to wait in the lobby. She started bitching, so again I told her to forget the whole thing. "Okay, okay," she said. "Just hurry up." But I took my time—partly just to piss her off, partly because I was having second thoughts and was hoping she'd get fed up and leave before I got back to the lobby. But for better or worse, she was still there when I came back down.

VIPs was one of the city's short-stay love motels—another great institution in Rio. VIPs was no fleabag hot sheet motel like those in New York, though. One time an old girlfriend of mine had convinced herself that screwing in one of those places would be romantic, so we checked into the Windjammer near my house. The place was so vile—cockroaches, stained pillowcases—I couldn't even get hard. VIPs was like the Waldorf Astoria by comparison. The suite came complete with a Jacuzzi, sauna, and a small dining room. In addition to snacks like peanuts and potato chips, a cabinet displayed condoms, KY Jelly, and sex toys for sale. All the suites had garages with private entrances. You could slip in and out without ever interacting with staff. A six-hour stay there cost about $30 in 2003.

Daniela demanded payment upfront, which was another red flag. All the free agents (i.e., non-terma girls) I'd been with had fucked first, collected after. Mongers on the boards file endless posts about this being an inviolable part of the protocol between garotas and clients. Watch out, they thunder, for any girl that tried to violate it.

I was more flexible in my thinking, though, so I offered her "half now, half when we leave." Again, she bitched a moment before finally agreeing. Thankfully, Daniela was well worth all her crap, at least in bed. If she harbored any anger toward me for not accepting her terms, it didn't manifest in a perfunctory performance. Perhaps she channeled the anger into her loins, because having sex with Daniela was like being devoured by a volcano.

Then, naturally, she reverted to form. As I was coming out of the bathroom, she was getting dressed. "What's up?" I asked. "Aren't we taking photos now?"

She responded with some shit about how she "thought we're going out to eat."

"What for?" I asked. "There's room service."

"Oh," she said, as if she didn't know that was an option. Meanwhile, she made for the door. Maybe I was still dazed from the sex, because I didn't know what she was up to. She was gone a good fifteen seconds before I had the sense to check inside my shoe, my brilliant hiding spot for the rest of her fee. The only thing left inside was lint.

If I wanted to catch her, I had no time to get dressed. So I ran after her in my underwear. She was at the far end of the lot getting into a cab. There were some hotel employees not far from her, and I yelled to them, "Thief! Stop her!"

They just scratched their heads. (Silly gringo! Are you that stupid?) The taxi took off.

She'd fucked me out of the photos and an all-nighter. But it was hard to be too upset after a fucking like that.

I paid the hotel bill and took a cab back to Terraco Atlantico, where I joined some working girls I'd befriended. Soon I spotted Daniela working a table of Americans. I walked over and said hello to her.

She smiled. "Hi Joe. *Tudo bem?*" ("Everything good?" It was Brazil's main greeting.) I was out for blood, but I didn't want to rile her up or create a scene. Daniela's English was decent, but not fluent, so I tried to lob hints over her head to the guys at the table. "Watch your assets," I said. "There's a shark in your midst."

She kept smiling, apparently clueless.

"Got it," one of the Americans responded. "Thanks."

I returned to my friends. A few minutes later, we heard a commotion coming from another table. It was the Americans chasing Daniela away. My laughter was interrupted by Daniela marching up to me, cursing and threatening. If I ever interfered with her work again, she said, she'd have her favela gangster brother kill me. I was tempted to remind her that she'd fucked me over first and to demand my money back (at least the half she'd stolen), but I decided that maybe it was better to be grateful that she'd given me a free pass this time. I had no idea if she could make good on her threat, but many of Rio's hookers come from the favelas, so I thought it wise to give her the benefit of the doubt.

I'd have to get the *Hustler* pictures somewhere else. Gabriella, another cutie with none of Daniela's malice, proved more reliable. We also went to VIPs for fucking and a photo shoot, both of which went off without incident. The sex with Gabriella wasn't anything remarkable, but she proved herself to be a surprisingly captivating model. Before we returned to Copacabana, she asked me to teach her come-ons she could use on other Americans. I tried to teach her "Come here, baby. I want to sex you up," but she couldn't say it without cracking up. It still worked on me, though, and we had sex one more time before leaving VIPs.

The next night I ran into Daniela again. Despite what had happened, she was pretty hot, so we went to a motel in Copacabana and spent the night together. I had to pay her again, but this time she didn't run off. I love to play with fire, I guess. Maybe the idea that she'd try to get revenge, that I was in some kind of danger, was exciting to me. Regardless, it's clear that Rio brings out the reckless moron in me.

A few days later, I bumped into Daniela again. She dragged me to an outdoor flea market near my hotel and demanded that I buy her jewelry. Instead, I bought her a two dollar T-shirt and told her to stop whining. I never slept with her again after that, but we've remained friendly toward each other. Now, when I visit Rio, she typically tries to grub drinks from me at Help. One time I said, "Buy *me* a drink for a change. You make more money than I do."

"Go fuck yourself, Joe," she said. But she came back a few minutes later and handed me a beer.

* * * *

Even with all the great shots I got of Gabriella, I was still short on photos for my *Hustler* article. With my trip coming to a close shortly, I feared that despite all the fun I'd been having, I'd end up regretting the trip if I didn't get paid for my article. So I hung around outside Help with my little three-megapixel click-and-shoot trying unobtrusively to shoot prostitutes. But some of them noticed and got livid. One girl sent a huge Brazilian man over to threaten my life if I didn't stop taking pictures of her.

In desperation, I hired an American photographer, Jack, who's among some very lucky sexpats, living the life of Riley in Rio. Jack's divorced, in his fifties, and not exactly *GQ* material. He seems to have a number of girls who sleep with him in exchange for him photographing them for their portfolios.

Jack told me about one of his lovers, Gina, a cute bisexual brunette. He said she had a very pretty lover, Jessie, and that maybe the two of them would be willing to pose for the magazine. Somehow he got them to do it for free, which was great. But not as great as the unexpected bonus the photo shoot yielded on my last night in town.

The four of us met outside Help before going to Jack's apartment. Jessie was a sultry blonde with black eyeliner and eyes like Elizabeth Hurley's. She didn't say much, and although I was excited that she'd agreed to do a photo shoot for my article, I didn't make much attempt to speak to her out of concern that the wrong thing might slip out of my mouth in broken Portuguese and make her change her mind.

But on the way to the apartment, Gina whispered to me that Jessie thought I was cute. I took the news with a grain of salt, but felt myself getting hard nonetheless.

To the growing lexicon of monger phraseology, let me add a term: *Lesbiana*. Not the "official" word, *lesbiana*, which is simply Portuguese (and Spanish) for lesbian. But my own contraction for a mythical place that existed so far only in my imagination: Lesbian Nirvana. (A nirvana as seen, of course, through a hetero male's point of view.)

My quest for Lesbiana is one of the driving forces behind my inability to be happy in a conventional relationship, or for that matter, a conventional career. It's why my cabinet is stocked with hundreds of lesbian porn films, most of which leave me cold. It's why no matter how often I learn that sex is usually better with just one girl, I can't give up the notion that the sexual paradise of my dreams is out there if I have enough balls to claim it.

If I had enough money, I'd rent a massive suite, or an auditorium, or a huge villa in Buzios, a resort area about a two-hour drive from Rio, and take the one hundred hottest bisexual girls or full-force lesbians I could find in Help and the termas, and let 'em rip.

If I had enough balls, I'd be directing my own line of all-girl orgy flicks by now. But I'm so much better at dreaming than at doing.

The girls went at it in Jack's bedroom. Gina looked too wholesome to really turn me on—I liked my girls a little bit naughtier. But there was a lot of fire between her and blonde-haired Jessie as Jack clicked away with his camera. They undressed each other and Jessie's tits were fantastic—a C cup at least with hard brown nipples that Gina licked over and over. Once Jessie's nipples were good and erect, Gina moved south. She licked Jessie's bare pussy clean, her tongue thrusting in and out while Jessie grabbed her hair and moaned. This was the stuff my dreams were made of. I didn't quite know what to do with myself. I was enjoying the show, but wasn't about to whip out my cock and start jerking off right there. In some vague way, I felt it was my job to supervise, since the shoot was for my article. I didn't give the girls much direction, though. Instead, I just hung back, overcome by a combined feeling of excitement and awkwardness— they didn't seem to notice I was there. At one point, I was sitting in the corner near the bed, still not knowing what to do with myself. After all, it was the first live lesbian show I'd ever seen.

Jessie looked at me teasingly every now and then. What's her game? I wondered. Gina or Jack had mentioned earlier that Jessie was a part-time hooker. Perhaps she was buttering me up for a session afterward? As the girls were finishing up, Jack told me that Jessie wanted me. I gazed over at her beautiful tanned breasts, her pert little cunt, and then back up to her sexy, black-rimmed eyes. What's her price? I asked. "Nada," he mouthed. When the girls were done, Jack and Gina headed for the foldout couch in his den. Jessie remained there, naked in bed. She spread her legs, waiting.

Wow. A hot bi babe giving me a freebie? And it was right around my birthday, too! What an incredible thrill. I honestly couldn't believe my good luck, and to show my appreciation, I gave her everything I had. I knew she'd just had Gina's tongue, so I figured she'd want something bigger and I went at her like a jackhammer. I bounced her up and down on my dick until I came, but she was strangely vacant the whole time—no dirty talk, no biting and not even a moan.

Turns out, everything I had wasn't enough, as afterward she excused herself for a moment. I waited in the bedroom for about ten minutes before stepping quietly into the den, where I found the three of them asleep on Jack's foldout. I gently pulled on Jack's leg. "What's going on?" I asked. "She said she'd be right back."

"That's pretty much it for the night," he said, before going back to sleep. Jessie's failure to return to the bedroom was likely a comment on my performance in bed, but I still judged the night a success. I had gotten decent photos for *Hustler*, and a surprise freebie that would make a nice finish to the article.

If I'd been more confident, I might have tried to stay in touch with Jessie. Who knows? She might have given me a chance to redeem myself the next time I was in town. Even better, she might have brought along other bi babes to join us. But here was one of the weird advantages of mongering: Why should I risk learning that a girl had no further interest in me, when I had access to countless women in Rio? Even if I had to pay them at first, there was a chance that there'd be another Juliana among them, and a more substantive relationship might evolve.

* * * *

I was a monger now, and at the very least, I could indulge my appetite for threesomes. I'd been fantasizing about *ménages à trois* since the first time I'd opened a porn magazine, and I was certainly willing to pay for a juicy encounter with the right pair of prostitutes.

As luck would have it, I was sitting at Terraco Atlantico one night when Beatriz, a fiery Latina I'd been with the night before, walked by. She'd been great in bed, but not because of any special technique. Instead, it was her spirit and intensity that took things to the next level. Girls like Beatriz made it incredibly easy to forget you were paying, to believe that she was enjoying it as much as you, and that there was no way she could be faking. And even if she was faking, she was so into her performance that she could probably derive some sort of artistic satisfaction in knowing just how good she was at it. With some Brazilian prostitutes, I think that's one of their goals besides making money. They want to not only give you a good time, but the best time you've ever had. And if that helps to make you a repeat customer, so much the better.

I waved Beatriz over to my table.

"Would you be up for sex with another girl?" I asked.

"Sure," she said. She sipped her drink nonchalantly, as if she were asked this every day by horny American guys like me. I couldn't tell if the idea truly appealed to her, or if she'd just go along with it for the sake of business. I pointed to a stunning black girl standing nearby who reminded me of Naomi Campbell.

"Do you know her?" I asked Beatriz.

"No. But she's very pretty."

"Why don't we talk to her and see if she's interested in a threesome?"

Beatriz winked at me; then she went over and brought the other girl back to the table. Her name was Sonia. I kept quiet while the girls spoke to each other in Portuguese. They seemed to hit it off, at least on a conversational level, so I decided to take them to a motel around the corner. Once we got there, I explained to them my ultimate lesbian fantasy, in which the girls start off devouring each other while ignoring me; or even better, tormenting me by "blowing me off" while they have euphoric sex with each other.

For the first few minutes, Beatriz and Sonia did their best to oblige. But Sonia quickly grew impatient, gesturing for me to join them.

"Please, keep going," I responded. But Sonia soon lost all traces of animation. I had sex with her, not out of any great desire, but in an attempt to restore the momentum. It was clear she didn't want to be there, so about halfway through the hour I told her it would be fine if she wanted to leave. I paid her and off she went. Beatriz and I agreed that Sonia was not the best choice for a threesome.

"*Tudo bem*," I said, as I started fucking Beatriz. If I learned anything from the experience, it's that these things need to be arranged with ample screening. When it comes to threesomes, looks don't matter as much as attitude, chemistry, and comfort level. And the more time you can spend beforehand with both girls together—talking, drinking, flirting—the better.

* * * *

By 2006, my skill at arranging threesomes had definitely improved. Joana was a regular at Help. She frequently wore jeans and a white T-shirt, which made her sexy in a tomboyish way. When I asked if she was into other women, her eyes lit up. In fact, she said, men were "just for work."

"I want this to be good," I told her. "I want us to pick a girl that we both like."

We "interviewed" a succession of about half a dozen girls at the club, but we couldn't agree on any of them.

"Come on," she urged. "Let's keep looking." Her dedication was a turn-on.

We spotted a prospective partner at the far edge of the dance floor near the stage. The girl was in her mid-to-late twenties, had a caramel complexion, and was wearing a tight, black, low-cut blouse. She didn't dance as much as she slithered. And when she stuck her tongue out at me, her stud caught the light and glimmered.

Joana and I approached her. As Joana explained our situation, Luciana kept smiling at me. At one point she grabbed my hand.

"Excuse us one second," I said to Luciana, stepping a few feet to the side with Joana.

"What do you think?" I asked.

"*Gostosa*," Joana said. "She's very sexy."

I was in total agreement.

"Are you really into women?" I asked Luciana.

She shrugged, raising a sexy eyebrow at me, and rubbed her fingers together making the international symbol for money.

She was gay for pay, the opposite of Joana. Ordinarily this would have been a deal-breaker, but Luciana had such a decadent quality about her that I asked her to come back with us anyway.

Luciana accepted my opening offer of $75 but on one very tantalizing condition. "When you're done with her," Luciana pointed to Joana, "I want you to fuck me."

She had to be kidding, I thought. What a tease!

"I can agree to that," I said.

I had one more piece of business to finish before we left Help. My friend Paulo, a Carioca who was celebrating his birthday that week, was talking to a prostitute, Priscila, upstairs. I offered to buy him a session as a gift, which he accepted, and the five of us headed back to my apartment. Luciana might not have been a true lesbian, but she put on one hell of a show kissing Joana in the elevator. They resumed their kissing in the apartment, even trying to get Paulo's girl involved. Priscila fooled around with them briefly, but wanted more money to join them in a full-on romp. Her request set off a chain reaction that nearly scuttled everything. First, it raised the issue of whether this was to become a bona fide orgy with Paulo joining in. Joana told me that in such a scenario, her and Luciana would also ask for more money. Trumping the financial considerations, though, was my disinclination to be anywhere near Paulo in bed. I love the guy, but he just doesn't fit into my vision of Lesbiana. Besides, I have a one-cock rule.

"Let's stick with our original plan," I said.

Paulo and his girl set up camp on the cot in the den (hey, I wasn't going to give him everything), while Luciana, Joana, and I took the bedroom. I explained my *torture-me-by-ignoring-me* fantasy, and the girls went at it vehemently, as if they were actual lovers. Perhaps they actually wished that I wasn't there, but it couldn't have been easy with me looking them up and down, side to side, moving my head like a camera, trying to catch their every move. Just as she had in the elevator, Luciana did everything with gusto—licking Joana's nipples, playing with her clit, and sucking on her tongue. I was starting to wonder if Luciana had lied about being straight, perhaps out of some misguided belief that I preferred my lesbians that way.

The more the girls got it on, the tougher I found it to keep my hands off. I wanted to screw both of them, but I knew Joana had no sexual interest in me. Luciana seemed to, however. She kissed me hard while Joana was going down on her.

I hadn't realized how long Joana and Luciana had kept at it. Before I knew it, there was a soft tapping on my bedroom door. "Yes?" I said, trying not to sound angry.

"Jo-ee," said Paulo through the door. "I'm sorry. But Priscila has to leave."

As I got up to pay her, Joana and Luciana took a breather. Joana said she needed to go too.

I asked Luciana if she could stay, and she said it wasn't a problem. Though I hadn't come, the threesome was still a visual feast that I had largely choreographed, like a director. The imagery would still have its practical use later on.

"What time do you need to go?" I asked.

She gave me a funny look, as if to say, "I could stay as long as you want me to."

"But I can't give you more money," I said.

"It's not a problem."

, This is why I love Rio.

We all got dressed and walked up the block toward the bus stop. It was sunrise, and we grabbed fresh-baked pastries at the bakery. "Don't forget," Luciana whispered in my ear. "You still have to fuck me."

We left Joana, Paulo, and Priscila at the bus stop and went back to the apartment. Now the sensations from the threesome, stored in my brain, had their afterlife. While fucking Luciana, I visualized every frame of her encounter with Joana, even their group kiss with Paulo's girl. Luciana rode me like she meant it, her tits bouncing up and down, sliding her hips up off my cock and then down hard again to meet my thrusts. The combination of Luciana's aggressive riding me on top and my recalling the ménage gave me an incredible orgasm. I have no idea whether her cries of *gostoso* had been sincere, but she kissed me passionately enough afterward to convince me she'd had fun too.

She'd convinced me enough that when we ran into each other the next night at Help, I was brimming with bravado. I cornered her against the wall, grinding her to the music without self-consciousness or the encouragement of liquor.

If I could dance that way and not feel like a fool (never mind what anyone else thought), then, I thought, I might as well speak the ludicrous words that had just formed in my head.

Looking right at Luciana, I said: "I can't afford you tonight, but go make some money and then, when you're done, we'll go back to my apartment and I'll fuck you the way you deserve to be fucked." I've rarely felt so cocky. She didn't laugh, throw her drink at me, or walk away. Instead, she gave me a long kiss, and then she waved goodbye. It was a good sign. An even better sign came when I saw her toward the end of the evening. Without so much as a word, she grabbed my fly and led me out the door, then fucked me for free.

CHAPTER FIVE

Pornaval

ONE OF THE ONLY TIMES I'VE MANAGED TO BREAK FREE OF RIO'S gravitational pull was around Carnival in 2004, when I arranged to cover a porn shoot in Buzios. The article, "Pornaval," was for *Fox* magazine which, despite their shared affection for tits and ass, has nothing to do with Fox Broadcasting. On the hardcore scale (with *Playboy* being the tamest, *Penthouse* being a bit raunchier, followed by a more-explicit *Hustler*), *Fox* was somewhere between *Hustler* and *Horse-Humpers*. I wrote frequently for *Fox*, mainly porn reviews and adventure stories like the one that led me to Buzios.

The film's producer, Third World Media, specialized in exotic sluts. Its signature lines included *Pretty Little Asians* and *Pretty Little Latinas*. These were high-quality fuck flicks, not the crap usually foisted upon fans of ethnic porn. The director, Ed Hunter, had a dream job shuttling between the Far East and South America. In Buzios, he rented a villa overlooking a beautiful lake. With its slice of private beach and high fences, the villa was the perfect place to shoot the latest edition of *Pretty Little Latinas*. "We bring everybody to these little resorts—very natural locations on the beaches, lakes, and rivers—and have a great time," Ed said. Who could resist that?

Still, it wasn't easy leaving Rio, even for a few days. I had a luxurious yet absurdly inexpensive oceanfront suite in Leblon at Motel Sinless. My mattress had ass prints from a variety of Help garotas I'd played with that week. Of course the Buzios trip would help me pay for all that debauchery. The manager agreed to hold my room until I returned.

The first actress I met at the villa was Deby, an adorable nineteen-year-old black girl with huge, luminous eyes. Sitting in the makeup chair, she looked a bit too wholesome for my tastes. But once she put on those gold leather shorts and matching bikini, I was enraptured.

"Where did you find her?" I asked Ed. His specialty was finding local talent. "We meet girls on the streets, and through contacts," he said. "These are real girls, not porn stars. Guys can go and meet them and fuck them themselves." In Brazil, that usually meant they were hookers.

In fact, I often had to remind myself that not every girl in Rio was in the sex trade. One time on the beach opposite Help, I'd been looking (all right, leering!) at a pair of pretty girls. One of them gave me a dirty look. I went over and asked why. She said she was on vacation from Portugal, and I had no right to assume she was a prostitute. I could have responded that she had no right to assume that I assumed she was a working girl. But she had me nailed. She knew exactly what I was thinking.

Here in Buzios, I wondered if I could score a freebie with Deby. The thought obsessed me the entire time.

She told me she planned to become a defense attorney.

"With your expertise, you can come to the U.S. and represent our hookers," I said.

"Why would they need a lawyer?" she asked. Like many Brazilians, she was shocked when I told her that prostitution wasn't allowed in the States.

My legal discourse was interrupted when Ed came over to introduce Victor, the lucky motherfucker who'd be nailing Deby in the first scene. That was enough reason to despise him. He was also carved from granite. I could work out for a thousand years and I'd never have a build like him. But he oozed charisma and it was impossible not to like him. He even helped me practice Portuguese, which could have improved my odds with Deby.

If sweet little Deby could survive this human Mac Truck, she was definitely cut out for porn. She kicked off the scene with a bit of booty-shaking for Ed's camera. She may have been skinny, but she had a full Brazilian butt and knew how to wiggle it. She also had a lovely set of natural tits. Not the kind of watermelons that I prefer, but absolutely perfect for her frame.

"What we try to do is have girls that are really natural, that really enjoy sex," Ed told me. "Girls that have real orgasms, that get fucked really hard. And these girls just love anal sex. They prefer it." Still, the thought of Victor in Deby's rectum made me uneasy. I don't like anal sex in my private life, and I wasn't crazy about watching it either. But I was there to do a job.

Deby went over to Victor, who was on the couch. Running his hands up and down her body, he commented on her assets. She played the nervous little virgin, whispering "no" as he ripped off her bikini. Victor slapped Deby's ass. "This girl has very beautiful body," he said, like a used-car salesman kicking the tires for a potential buyer.

If Deby had any initial nervousness she got over it fast, cooing as Victor munched on her clit. Then she got on all fours, giving his fingers easy access to her anus. Her coos dropped down the sonic register into throaty moans.

Next, while giving Victor head, she turned slightly toward the camera and gave a smile (a pretty good one, I must say, considering the circumstances). I was standing by the camera at the time, and my imagination got the best of me. *Was her smile aimed at me?* I wondered. *Why was she so happy? Could it be that she was imagining me having sex with her instead of Victor?*

Meanwhile, the real test of Deby's intestinal fortitude began. After Victor was through with her butt, would she have to wear adult diapers for the rest of her life? I don't know if she was an anal virgin, but she certainly didn't cave in under the pressure. Instead, she oohed and aahed through the whole thing. Ed was delighted with her performance. In a sick way, I was proud of her. Or at least relieved. It would have been a hell of a lot worse if she'd run off in agony.

The next actress, Isabella, looked liked Susanna Hoffs. Remember her from the Bangles? (I sure do; I wanked off to her poster many times.) Isabella, making her porn debut, had long black hair, and full red lips that were ideal for this line of work. I would have been "smitten" with her too, if Deby hadn't conquered me first.

Or had she? A few seconds after Ed yelled "Action," Isabella spread her labia to reveal a "roast beef" pussy; dark on the outside, tender pink on the inside. If I'd had some honey mustard, they would have needed the Jaws of Life to pry me off her.

I was happy, though. If I couldn't have her, at least my man Victor, all rested from his tango with Deby, would be my surrogate. His on-screen rival for Isabella's favors would be Jax, whom I drove up with from Rio. Jax didn't speak any English, but he was always smiling, as if he couldn't believe how much God had smiled on him with this job (if you could even consider getting paid to fuck hot Brasileiras a job).

For now, his job was to engage Isabella in some classic sixty-nine. Isabella's hair kept falling in her eyes. She was fine, though, operating on pure animal instinct. She screamed "*Gostoso!*" the Portuguese word for delicious. "*Gostoso!*" (The word can also be used to express intense pleasure, so I'm not sure if she was reacting to the taste of Jax's pole, or his tongue in her twat.)

Jax then proceeded to play butt-bongo on her ass, giving Isabella's cheeks a fresh glow. Then the three of them attempted something pretty severe for a first-time porn girl like Isabella. Victor and Jax mounted her front and back in a double-penetration. Her cries of "*Gostoso!*" were shattering. I had to cover my ears. If I were a really nice boy, I would have covered my eyes, too.

When the day's shooting was over, I hoped to spend time flirting with Deby. But because she had no more scenes to shoot, she was headed back to Rio that night to work at her other job. She did online strip shows for a website called RioFantasyChat.com. (I never found out whether she was also a bona fide hooker.) I tried to convince her to stay. "Baby, I'm so sorry," she said. Apparently, she had a regular client, a foreign gentleman, who paid her a shitload just to see her writhe around on his monitor. Of course, there was no guarantee she'd end up with me had she stayed, but who knows? Anyway, I liked hanging out with her. She was refreshing. Innocence and decadence all wrapped up in a single mouthwatering package.

I was too stimulated to stay in Buzios. The place was paradise for couples, but no place for single guys like me. This was Brazil, damn it. You don't get blue balls in Brazil. I had enough material for the article. It was a tribute to Ed's porn-meister skills that I was so worked up. If I had to watch from the sidelines as another hot girl got fucked, my testicles would explode. I had to get back to Rio. He understood.

CHAPTER SIX

We'll Always Have Rio (Betina)

I'VE MET SOME OF THE MOST EXTRAORDINARY WOMEN AT HELP Discoteca, though the place wasn't always kind to me. After I returned from Buzios, I starting noticing a girl at Help each night with jet black hair and Mediterranean features. Her only imperfection was a slightly hawkish nose. She'd walk around erect as a model as if she owned the place. I imagined her playing rough with me in bed, just the way I liked it, but every time I'd try to make eye contact she'd give me a dirty look. She radiated bitchiness. Naturally, I had to meet her.

One night I saw her flirting with a group of Americans. As always, she looked glamorous and unapproachable in high heels that accentuated her well-toned calves. She wore a short black dress that clung to her chest. In a sea of Carnival-clad garotas decked out in gaudy sequins, her dress stood out for its simplicity.

The guys who were talking to her seemed to be in good spirits, and I had enough *caipivodka* in me (no more caipirinhas for this monger; I hate cachaça) to approach them. It's something of an unwritten rule among gringos at Help that guys are friendly to each other. There are too many "available" women to worry about cockblocking. And if the other guy goes with the one you want tonight, you can always have another chance with her tomorrow.

Of course, I was hoping to use these Americans to establish a bridgehead to the girl, and fortunately they introduced me to her. Not only was Betina cordial, she spoke English well to boot. The Americans eventually wandered off, but I doubt it was because I'd moved in on their territory. It's far more likely that they were just in a "let's flirt with everyone" mood.

I hung out with Betina, and to my surprise learned that she wasn't a bitch. She wasn't sweet like candy, but she was extremely engaging, seemingly interested in everything I said.

I offered her a drink, and she asked for a vodka with "hedgee bull."

"Hedgee bull?" I scratched my head.

"I'm sorry. Red Bull."

It's one of the peculiarities of Brazilian Portuguese that Cariocas pronounce the letter D at the end of a word with a "gee" sound. "How is business here tonight?" I asked. She knew what I meant. But she said she wasn't working tonight.

"So what brings you to Help?" I asked.

"Just because I'm off-duty, it doesn't mean I don't have certain needs," she responded with a wink.

I'm sure any guy in the club that night would have volunteered to fill those needs, especially if they knew that her price for that night was zero. For the life of me, I couldn't figure out why she was letting me in on her agenda. I gathered she was just being nice, having a few drinks with me, until a man worthy of a freebie (or her knight in shining armor) came along.

But I guess there's no predicting the rules of attraction. We sat out on the veranda overlooking Copacabana Beach. I told her I really wanted to spend the night with her. "How much would it cost?" I asked, having filtered out what she'd said about being off-duty.

"That's the first stupid thing you've said all night, Joe. I told you: I'm not working."

As I tried to apologize, she started walking away.

"I'm so sorry," I said. "It's loud in there. I didn't quite understand what you'd said."

"I'm just going to the bathroom," she said. "I'll be back."

How many times had I heard *that* before? As the minutes passed, that feeling of dread grew in my stomach. *How did I fuck this one up?* I wondered. What was her game, giving me dirty looks the other nights, being nice to me tonight, only to blow me off in the end?

Oh me of little faith. She returned.

"I thought I'd really pissed you off," I said.

"No, Joe. Not at all. I enjoy talking to you."

"I'd like to be with you tonight."

Someone brushed the back of my hair. Betina was smiling. I turned around to see Camila, a girl I'd slept with a few nights earlier. She was wearing a silver sequined bikini and feather headdress for Carnival.

"Hi, Joe," she said. "*Tudo bem?*"

I smiled. "Very good," I said. The thought of a threesome immediately crossed my mind, but it was not to be.

Camila blew me a kiss. "Okay, baby" she said. "Have fun."

"You like Brazil," Betina said. "Yes, Joe?"

I didn't want to seem too enthusiastic. "It's nice here," I answered.

"Why do American men like it here so much?"

I squirmed, then tried to joke my way out of saying what we both knew was the only honest answer. "I think it's the churros," I said, referring to the pastries sold by pushcart vendors throughout the city.

She laughed.

"I can't find those things in New York," I joked. "That's the only reason I come here."

She kicked me gently under the table. "Stop, Joe. You're very silly. What about your friend?" she asked, gesturing toward Camila by the door.

"Rio is a dream world for me," I said. "I'm able to do things here that I never experience at home."

"This is the real world for me," Betina responded.

"I know. I want to stay with you tonight."

"I don't know," she said. "You're going home in a few days."

"Why is that bad?"

"I don't want to start liking someone who's leaving soon."

If it had been a ploy to get more money out of me, it would have worked. But Betina, a widow with a young son who was trying to launch a craft and jewelry design business, didn't strike me as a member of the hardened-hustler camp.

"I come to Rio a lot," I said. "If we hit it off, we can see each other again. But that's in the future. Life can only be lived one second at a time. Why don't we just take it one second at a time and see what happens?"

If I'd had more guts, I would have said it while grabbing her hand and gazing into her eyes. But she didn't seem inclined to make me jump through flaming hoops.

"Come on," she said. "*Vamos*?"

We went back to my suite at Motel Sinless, possibly the most ironically named place in Rio. Sinless was another "love motel" in Leblon, similar to VIPs, where I'd taken Daniela. Although the motel was intended for short stays, I was staying there the whole trip. Scoring the suite had been a stroke of inspiration. I'd waited to the last minute to try to book a hotel, and wasn't yet sold on the advantages of renting a private apartment. Hotel prices during Carnival were outrageous. Then I'd had a brainstorm: VIPs had only cost me about $30 for a six-hour stay my last time there; a twenty-four-hour stint would still be a bargain at that rate. Maybe I could book it for my entire trip. VIPs wasn't available, but Sinless was. So for a fraction of the cost of a regular hotel, I got to stay in a luxurious oceanfront suite with a Jacuzzi, sauna, and a huge shower.

When Betina and I arrived, the first thing I did was slip into the bathroom to pop a Cialis that I'd bought over the counter at a pharmacy in Copacabana. (Isn't Brazil wonderful?) An earlier experience with Viagra that I will describe later had convinced me of the usefulness of these drugs. Cialis lasted longer than Viagra, thirty-six hours versus four hours. I had no hang-ups about either pill being an "old man" drug. My view had been reinforced when I'd gone to a brothel in Copa with a few porn actors who'd been filming in Rio. I'd been surprised when they'd made a detour to a drug store to purchase some packages of penile pick-me-ups. Both men were in their late twenties and were in excellent shape.

"Why did you get Cialis?" I asked.

"For the edge," one of them replied.

I'm not sure how much credit goes to the Cialis, but Betina and I had a great time in bed. In my increasingly "maverick" worldview, it was a watershed moment for me—Betina was the first (and still, only) Brazilian prostitute that went with me right off the bat for free. It was one of those "this is why I come to Rio" moments, like my first kiss with Juliana.

In my mind, at least, I occupied a higher perch than all those mongers who'd paid for what they got. It was the equivalent of dating a hot stripper back in the States, which I've never done—though not from lack of trying. I'd hung out a few times with strippers when they weren't working and paid for dinner or drinks. But not even a peck on the cheek resulted, so they hardly qualified as the kind of "dates" I'd been hoping for. My ambition has changed over the years from wanting to be a famous crusader against crime, to having an exotic dancer (or porn star) trophy girlfriend. I don't see it so much as lowering my sights as readjusting them to humbler goals—goals that still might not be humble enough in my case.

Not long ago, my friend Scott asked why I seemed to have an easier time starting "relationships" with Brazilian pros than with American civilian girls. It was a great question. I think that to succeed in their job, prostitutes have to be naturally more open to the different types of guys who approach them. The girls there can't automatically be as "choosy" if they want to make money. They might prefer a guy who looks like a male model, but they can't limit themselves to that. In a New York City bar, an attractive girl has her pick; she can think to herself, "I'll talk to him, but not him. That guy, yes. But not the guy next to him." With a garota de programa, though, I can start from a position of strength without having to sweat over how "good" I look that night. Once I'm able to display a little charm and self-confidence, the girl might find herself with a growing attraction to me that transcends my wallet. Though she wasn't seeking clients, Betina was probably already open-minded in this way. Then again, despite all my insecurities about my looks, maybe she just found me cute and things progressed from there. After all, Juliana had also approached me just from me gazing at her.

Betina and I spent my last few days in Brazil together. She came with me to the airport. On the way there, she gave me a gift, a blue candle that she'd made, topped off with a plastic angel. When she cried in my arms at the gate, I felt like Bogie at the end of Casablanca.

We stayed in touch over the phone. At first, I loved hearing her voice. But when the excitement faded, I realized how hard it was for us to understand each other on the phone. Even now, when my Portuguese is pretty damn good, calls to Brazil are a bitch. I don't know if it's my long-distance carrier, my phone, or the Brazilian telecommunications system, but the signal quality is never steady. And nothing on the phone makes up for body language. Betina and I could communicate fine in person, but our phone conversations were tortuous. I have enough trouble sustaining romances with local girls. After a month or so, Betina and I stopped calling each other.

Still, thinking about her—especially the airport goodbye—was enough to keep me primed for another visit. Within a few months I booked a flight for August. As the date approached, I tried to call her, but the line was disconnected. Okay, I thought. It would give me a chance to really get into Bogie mode: I could play Sam Spade and track her down when I got to Rio.

It wasn't easy. Betina had once shown me her apartment building, but I didn't remember the address. I knew the general vicinity, at the southern edge of Copacabana, near the Alvim Tunnel and the Cantagalo favela. So I spent an afternoon canvassing the area, asking doormen in any building that looked like hers if they knew Betina. The problem was that all the apartments looked like her building: rows of attached non-descript apartment complexes behind security gates, sandwiched between the tiny stores and rundown lunch counters that constituted much of the commercial activity at that end of Copa.

Finally, I found her building, but the doorman said she'd moved about a month earlier.

I had one other lead to pursue. On my previous trip, I'd gone with Betina to pick her son up at school. Again, I didn't remember exactly where it was, but I roamed around Copacabana looking for it. No luck. A few days later, I tried again. This time I found a school that seemed familiar, but I wasn't sure. My best bet would be keeping an eye out for Betina when school let out. Now I just had to find out what time that would be.

The principal was a friendly woman in her fifties. I explained that I was hoping to run into "a friend from my last visit. I think her son goes here." Too late, the thought struck me, *was I insane?*

A guy by himself, clearly not from the community, inquiring about dismissal time for small children?

In the States, that would have been enough to set off alarm bells. I tensed up, anticipating an even more vehement reaction here, a school in one of the most dangerous cities on earth. But the principal simply asked, "What's the name of your friend and her son?"

To my surprise, she confirmed that Betina's little boy, Juninho, went there. She even let me know what time he'd be getting out. Maybe this nice lady was the one that ought to be arrested, I thought. I was unshaven, wearing my finest gringo-vagabond clothes. Maybe I didn't look as rugged or as much of an outlaw as I thought. Maybe all she saw was a harmless dweeb.

I had about an hour until the school let out, so I raced to my apartment, showered and shaved, and raced back. There I saw Betina sitting in a doorway opposite the building, reading a book. I stopped a few feet in front of her, and cleared my throat so she'd look up.

Betina did a double take. *"Meu dios,"* she said as she broke into a huge smile.

Such things defy time. Her warm reaction made meaningless all the credit card debt I was piling up on these trips.

We hugged, and suddenly things were exactly how we left off at the airport. Resuming the relationship seemed effortless.

We quickly became what seemed like a normal couple: taking her son to the beach; food shopping; going out for dinner; taking moonlit strolls around Copacabana Beach (there's nothing like taking your life in your hands to get the adrenaline pumping); fucking every night. It only took several days for the same old shit that had destroyed my other relationships to surface. I'm like a heart-transplant recipient who responds beautifully at first, romance like new life pumping through my veins. But then my body rejects the implant, and I become increasingly uncomfortable in the relationship.

Like Jerry Seinfeld's character on *Seinfeld*, who would obsess over a girl's "man hands" or some other absurd flaw until he couldn't stand to be near her, I found myself thinking more and more about the little bump on Betina's nose, to the exception of everything else.

Rio is not the best place to overcome commitment phobia. Much to the contrary, it's a place for indulging it, reveling in it. I was walking toward Meia Pataca when I saw Estela, a girl I'd picked up at Help on my first night back in Rio. Estela was a redheaded pixie who liked to wear tight shorts and low-cut blouses. She had a caressing voice and was a great kisser. I wanted to fuck her again, but I was in a relationship—even if it was quickly growing stale—with Betina. We were supposed to meet up in a few hours. Would it really be so bad to cancel one date with Betina? It was like weighing whether or not to run a red light late at night when the streets are deserted. Even if a cop in hiding catches you, you really haven't violated the spirit of the law, which is to prevent accidents. Right? Ditching Betina for Estela wouldn't be cheating, I reasoned. Whatever Betina's feelings for me, both women were still prostitutes. And even though I knew I was wrong, and that there was no way I could rationalize what I was considering, I went right ahead and did it anyway.

Feigning intoxication, I called Betina about a half hour before our date, telling her that I'd been drinking at my friend's apartment and was going to stay there and sleep it off. She told me to go to my apartment and wait for her. There was no problem with the sound quality on this call, but I made believe that I couldn't understand her.

Nervously, I collected Estela and grabbed a cab to Sinless. I was able to turn my guilt off long enough for Estela to drive me nuts in bed. She brought me close to orgasm over and over again with her mouth and I forgot all about Betina. Just as I was about to explode from those sexy lips pumping up and down my cock, Estela would pause and leave me wanting more. The anticipation was almost unbearable, but as she sucked me off, her round ass up in the air, I thought about what a lucky bastard I was. When I couldn't stand it anymore, I flipped her over and fucked her until I came.

How easy it was to feel "magic" with her too. But, I still found time that night to let guilt wash over me, lying anxiously in bed, staring silently into space. When Estela asked what was wrong, I confessed how awful I felt about screwing over Betina. I'm not sure if I wanted to impress Estela with a brave display of honesty about my faults, or drive her away by emphasizing my shortcomings.

When I was in my mid-twenties, my girlfriend had asked me whether it was her I loved or if I was "just passionate with girls in general." Although there are worse things to admit to oneself, I had preferred to believe the former. But Brazil was doing its best to prove otherwise. For someone who's comfortable in his own skin, who has made peace with his inability to settle down, Brazil *can* be the setting for an ideal life. One can have his soul mate, and whenever he feels restless, he can bust out for a few hours and choose from an endless stream of prostitutes.

Of course, to pull it off regularly, you also need some finesse. Certainly more than I'm usually capable of mustering.

When I returned to Copa in the morning, I called Betina.

"I waited at your apartment for hours," she said.

I tried to stay consistent with my alibi from our last call. "I was too drunk. I stayed at my friend's."

She knew I was full of shit. "Don't call me again," she said. "You're just going to keep hurting me."

I let her hang up without an argument, resisting the urge to call her back.

None of it's real, I tried to convince myself. There was no need for me to give into remorse or guilt or sadness at having driven away another woman who found meaning in being with me. Ultimately, I guess I had been playing at being her boyfriend. The times we'd spent with her son were like playing at being a father. Maybe that's how Rio's prostitutes should market themselves: A GFE combined with what you might call an *FHE* (Fatherhood Experience). All the lines were beginning to blur.

My screwup with Betina notwithstanding, I tend to be more "monogamous" when it comes to my relationships in Rio. As long as the feeling of intimacy lasts, it's a lot more cost-effective, and emotionally less confusing, to stay with the same girl. Still, I'm thrilled that on the other side of the ledger, I've had more meaningless trysts with Brazilian hookers than I can remember. I know: quite an achievement. Right up there with winning an Olympic medal or removing a brain tumor. But even if it does nothing to advance civilization, sometimes I feel just as happy from a good lay as I did when I fought against rapists getting parole. It's all subjective.

Logically, it shouldn't even do anything for the ego. Buying a gold medal is not the same as earning it. How to account for the thrill, then? Imagine a kid repeatedly riding a roller coaster. It's not much of an accomplishment, athletic or otherwise. But there's a cumulative charge that comes from knowing that you've done it so many times. Also, strangely enough, guys seem to respond with as much gusto to your tales of sleeping with hookers as to your actual "conquests" with civilian girls. Probably because your "ability" to go with a prostitute is no threat to your friends' egos. They can just as easily "conquer" a hooker as you can. At the same time, society places great value on how you spend your money. Some art collectors get as much praise as the artists whose work they collect.

* * * *

I'd have one more encounter with Betina before it was all over.

The night I arrived on my next visit to Rio in November 2004, I went to Help immediately after dropping off my stuff at the apartment. Betina was near the drink-ticket booth. She had a halter dress on, a red version of the white one Marilyn Monroe made famous. Betina and I stared at each other. I hesitated before going over. *Should I kiss her hello?* I wondered. *Where? On the lips. No, that wouldn't be right.* I played it safe with a peck on her cheek. She slurred something about it being her birthday—didn't I want to give her a real kiss? I would love to have given her a real kiss, but what right did I have after making such of mess of things the last time? Still, she kept looking at me. Then she grabbed me and pulled me toward her. We started kissing. She shoved me away, then pulled me back in. Yes. No. Yes. No. It was the kind of crazy passion I rarely encountered at home. Am I a sadist? Maybe. I liked seeing her struggle with herself over wanting to kiss me. But really, I'm a masochist. I liked that she had me struggling with myself over what was the right thing to do—the monger versus the kid who always held the door for his older neighbors. Push. Pull. Push. Pull. We were tangled up in each others' yo-yo strings.

Her friend came over, a girl I didn't know. She asked me to keep an eye on Betina. I had to think that through. We were both on an emotional high wire that demanded extreme caution. Betina seemed so sad. Was it really her birthday? As much as I thought I'd learned about her, as well as other prostitutes I'd known in Rio, this underscored how little I really knew. I'd always thought Betina was so on top of things. But here she was, drunk and lonely, on what should have been a night of celebration for her.

We were right near Help's "vomit spot," a small area by the bar that perpetually reeked. She was shaky on her feet, so I steadied her against the bar.

I had no right to complicate her life further, but I also didn't want to just walk away or see her sad or let her meet some even bigger asshole who'd treat her even worse than I had. If she wanted to make money that night, I certainly had no right to interfere with her ability to earn, regardless of the nature of her work. I backed away in baby steps, hoping I could at least look out for her from a growing distance. Betina seemed fine for a few seconds, didn't seem to notice my retreating. Then she glared at me. "You're just going to leave me on my birthday?" she asked, incredulously. I went back to her, close enough so she could hear me over the music. "I don't know what to do," I said. "I want to stay with you. But you're angry with me. Which you should be. I don't want to fuck up your birthday."

I touched her ponytail and she swatted my hand away. I started apologizing, but she interrupted me with a kiss. Yes. No. Yes. No. Her friend returned. "She's too drunk," the friend said. "Please, take her out of here." Maybe the friend was trying to expedite an offer from me to Betina. But she seemed to know I was Betina's ex-flame, and her concern seemed genuine.

I got Betina out by putting my arm around her and easing her forward without looking directly at her. The less I look, the less I'll provoke her, I figured. Just keep her focused on walking. She won't be able to think of anything else.

Once outside, I didn't know what to do. My internal wrestling match resumed. Should I persuade her to come back to my apartment? Should I get her safely back to hers and say goodnight? In the end, I chose the middle ground—burgers at Bob's. As we ate out back, she began to sober up.

"Why are you here?" she asked.

"I'm in Rio for . . ."

"No. Why are you here with *me*?"

I couldn't say what I was thinking: that I loved being with her. That I loved this moment. Loved that she couldn't keep her hands off of me. That she was ravenous for me.

I said I wanted to make sure she got out of Help all right.

"This is no good. You're going to hurt me again."

I wish I could have said to her that we should just take it one second at a time, as I had the night we met. But the words didn't occur to me this time.

"Betina, I don't want to hurt . . . "

"Please, go. I shouldn't have come here with you."

I sat, fidgeting, hoping for a reprieve. "Please," she repeated.

Playful teasing is one thing, but it's another thing entirely to realize that you're causing anguish to someone you like by your very presence. I also knew that I had nothing long-term to offer her or her son. Though with enough charm and persistence, I might have short-circuited her wariness long enough to reignite her appetite for me.

Then we could have gone on and had great make-up sex. Which could have led to us dating again. Which could have led to more sex. But each time with less passion. Until, finally, I'd run like hell again.

No. Betina's way was the right way. I nodded at her and walked off toward my building, looking back now and then to make sure she was okay. I spent many subsequent nights scouring Help for her, but I never saw her again. As with Juliana, I hope that she met a good man, a good father for Juninho.

CHAPTER SEVEN

Lorena Bobbitt/The First Cut Is the Deepest

It took me many trips to Rio to finally figure out that just about everyone in Copacabana's sex trade knows each other. If you plan on returning—and you will—you don't want to needlessly alienate anyone, regardless of your level of interest in the person. The trick, of course, which I have yet to master, is smiling politely in a non-committal way. Also, keep in mind that, despite your best efforts at diplomacy, the more time you spend in Copacabana, the more "enemies" you'll create among the working girls. There are two reasons: First, some girls that you're not attracted to will either repeatedly approach you, or wonder why you never approach them; no matter how nice you are in general, some of them will come to resent you. It's not your fault; if the shoe was on the other foot and you keep hitting on a girl in the States, would she "owe" you anything just because you were interested in her? Still, this can become a problem for you in Rio if the girl decides to badmouth you around Copa.

Secondly, ex-girlfriend garotas are a source of potential friction in Copa. It doesn't matter whether it's a working girl with whom you had a bona fide romance, or for whom you were merely a sugar daddy. The important thing is how the relationship ended. One of the girls I'd been involved with, Aline, had stopped charging me at some point, only to resume asking for money later on.

Her request caught me off guard, because not long before she'd written me, "My Love Joey, I want to please you beyond words. And more still I want to simply occupy your glance. I want to touch your soul and move your heart, to the point that the memory of me stays marked always in your thoughts." There was no way she was interested in my money, I'd convinced myself.

So I ended it. "I won't go back to paying you," I told her. Before I knew it, I was getting dirty looks on a regular basis from about nine or ten prostitutes in Copa.

"*Que pasa?*" I asked one of them, whom I recognized as Aline's friend.

She said that Aline had told them I was a cheapskate and a "bad guy." Luckily for me, I was somewhat able to repair my image by spending an afternoon with a few of the girls at Meia Pataca buying them drinks and food.

Of course, it's easier to be "charming" with a new girl who hasn't been stirred up against you. One afternoon I was sitting by myself outdoors at Meia Pataca. There was no sun, and not much of a crowd, just a few scattered gringos and garotas. A blonde with a ponytail smiled at me. She had a touch of acne, but it didn't diminish how cute she was. The problem was she only looked seventeen or eighteen. "Not for me," I thought, flashing her a smile in response, then quickly turning away.

I tried to keep myself focused on nothing in particular. I wrote a bit in my "journal" (i.e., napkins and scraps of paper), mainly to avoid glancing at her. That didn't work for long. I had to know if she was still looking at me; I had to know if she was interested in me ("interested" of course being a relative term in a pay-for-play environment). Every time I looked over, there she was, still smiling.

I kept this little game going for a while, hoping that a girl more to my tastes would show up. None did, so I invited the blonde over to my table. Her name was Lisa, and she was from Porto Alegre, near Brazil's southern border with Uruguay.

"I'm only in Rio a few days," she said. "I want to earn some money before I go back to university."

"How?" I asked. "Making the program?"

"Of course," she said.

I liked it when working girls were upfront about their activities. Many of them were, either because they realized how obvious it was in these circumstances, or they were just too guileless to act like hardcore hustlers, the kind who think that they could get your money without you knowing that you were "hooked." Lisa radiated guilelessness, which made her presence in Copa all the more intriguing. No matter how many "innocent" girls with an ineradicably wholesome vibe I'd met in Rio's sex trade, they always seemed incongruous in such a place.

"You don't seem anything like a program girl," I said.

"I'm really not. Just till I start university again."

"What are you studying?" I asked.

"International relations," she said.

I almost fell out of my chair. It was the perfect parallel to her current job, keeping foreign tourists happy. "Do you get credit for your 'field work' here in Rio?" I asked.

Lisa was sharp. She got the joke. She got all my jokes, damn her!

I don't want anybody to think that I fall in love at the drop of a hat. That said, I can become smitten in a heartbeat. Give me a cute, friendly girl who makes good conversation and knows how to flirt, and I'm spellbound. America is filled with women like that. They're in almost any large nightclub, office, supermarket, or shopping mall. Still, my ability to connect with women in the States has always been inconsistent. The vastly different social dynamics of Rio—that mix of native sensuality running through the veins of attractive women with "middle-class" traits engaged in legal prostitution in places and at prices that are accessible to the average American—make it so much simpler for me to connect with women on a variety of levels.

Yet I was still lucky to meet Lisa, and I knew it. True, I've had similar luck other times in Brazil, like with Juliana and Betina, but those encounters have been the exception. That, of course, is what makes them so special. I'm sad to say I don't remember much about most of the pros I've slept with. I don't have a mental picture of every vagina, every set of tits, or every perfect ass I've ever fucked. What I remember, as a monger, are the women who talked to me like I was a real man. This book focuses on the exceptions because, naturally, they were more exceptional and their stories more worthy of retelling. But I've had enough extraordinary experiences with women in Rio to decide that Rio itself, warts and all, is magical.

It's like Vegas to a pro gambler: he might lose more rounds than he wins, but his overall take is phenomenal.

I still had little desire to sleep with Lisa at that point. The age thing (at least how young she looked) was just too off-putting.

"I have to ask you, how old are you?"

"Nineteen," she replied. I gave her a skeptical look.

"I don't have my document with my age, but I can get it from my apartment if you want," she said.

"It's not necessary. I'm not really looking to go with someone today."

"Oh," she said. "Why not?"

"I think I've had too much sex already." (I'd had sex twice that morning already, and was feeling like I wanted to relax.) "I need to just sit here in Meia Pataca and rest for a month."

"Yes, you look very old," she teased.

"Also, I think you're adorable," I said. "But I think of you more like a little sister than someone I would sleep with." With our respective ages, "daughter" might have been more accurate to say than "sister," but that would have been too depressing for me.

She didn't seem offended. I, on the other hand, was consumed with guilt, as if I'd just run over a puppy. I nervously kept repeating how cute she was, how smart and charismatic, and that I was sure she would do great business here. I had handed her a perfect out for her to excuse herself and look for other clients; I was glad when she didn't take it.

"I have to go around the corner and check my email and do some errands," I said. "Do you want to come with me?"

"I thought you don't want to stay with me."

"It's complicated," I said. "I don't want to take you away from work. I like being with you. But I don't think it's a good idea if we have sex. I can't pay you if you come with me, but I'll take you for dinner later. And we can go to a movie or something, if you like."

She nodded, flashing that cute smile again.

As we walked around Copacabana, my thoughts inevitably turned where I didn't want them to. "Hypothetically," I said with great emphasis, "how do the think the sex between us would be?"

"Why?"

"Well, I guess I'm curious," I said. "You've spent the whole afternoon with me even though you know I can't be your client. Let me ask you, and please be honest. Do you think I'm attractive?"

"I think you're very nice," she said.

"Do you kiss clients?"

Lisa thought for a moment. "Sometimes. Depends how attracted I am."

"What about me? Would you kiss me?"

"I'm not sure—not to hurt you, but probably not."

By all rights, I should have taken her response at face value and let the matter rest, but instead I raised the ante.

"Trust me," I said. "You'd kiss me."

She shrugged, as if to say, "If that's what you want to believe . . . "

My need to prove my awesomeness was overtaking my sensible caution about her age. I was going to kiss her, damn it, and she was going to like it. Or at the very least I would find out if she was full of shit about not wanting to suck face.

Sure enough, I soon found myself playing Let's Make a Deal with Lisa. And by then I was too charged up to wait while she went to her apartment to get her ID. Fuck it! She's legal, I reassured myself. Or more precisely, I let concerns about her age float away from me.

We agreed on $60 for two hours, and went to my apartment. As we fooled around, I kissed her everywhere but her lips. Here was a "trick" I'd learned long ago: Kiss all around her neck and mouth. On the cheeks, earlobes, chin, forehead. Even the nose. Then slow down a bit to see how she responds. I also made sure to caress the back of her neck.

Her jaw muscles loosened, her lips parted, and out popped her tongue like a tiger cub seeking someone to play with. *Aha*, I thought. *I got her!*

Now I could move down her tight body into more dangerous territory, giving her oral. Meantime, she reached into my briefs and played with my dick.

"Why are these still on?" she asked.

"I don't know. I just didn't get around to taking them off yet."

"Well, take them off," she demanded.

"First you have to earn it," I teased. It was great feeling this comfortable with someone. She played with my dick some more, grinding herself into me as she pressed me against the wall.

Soon, breathless, she told me to fuck her.

"Maybe," I said.

"Huh? Maybe?"

"Yeah, maybe." As I was saying it, I wanted to make sure she knew that I was just goofing around, and that I was turned on like mad. I fingered her, hoping it was deft enough to be pleasant. She was soaking wet and dripping all over my hand.

"But don't worry," I added. "I'm still going to pay you even if we don't fuck." That part I meant. It was a litmus test I'd thought up on the spot. If her interest was mainly money, she could have stopped right then and I would have paid her in full.

"You better fuck me," she said, rising and falling against my hand as I finger fucked her, hard, both of us still standing up.

"If you don't fuck me . . . " Lisa pulled her upper body back from me and made a scissors gesture, smiling like one of Dracula's wives and then looking down at my penis. It was rock hard, and I didn't want to lose either my hard on, or my dick! What could I do? I didn't want to end up like John Wayne Bobbitt, so I gave in. I threw her on the bed and rammed my dick where my fingers had been moments before, her pink thong panties shoved to the side. She was a screamer, it turned out—not as shy in bed as she was in public. My dear sweet Lisa must have woke everyone in the building, and damn is that good for the ego.

We hung out for a few days afterward, mostly horizontally. Just before she left to go home, she caught up with me at Meia Pataca, and pulled out a document from her pocketbook. "A surprise," she said as she handed it to me.

I could immediately tell that it was an ID. I scanned it quickly for her age, fearing I was about to discover I'd committed a major crime. Maybe she planned to blackmail me. Maybe a detachment of police were about to spring forth from the bushes.

The document said she was born in 1981. This was 2005, and it took me forever to do the simple math and determine that she was twenty-four.

"Why did you tell me you were nineteen?" I asked.

"Because many Americans don't like older girls," she said.

"Not me," I laughed. "This is the best surprise you could have given me. Twenty-four is a perfect age."

Truth is, I had taken a stupid risk and lucked out. She just as easily could have been a minor and my mongering days might have ended behind bars.

I've stayed in touch with Lisa, though we haven't seen each other again. I'm not clear if she's still in college; last time we spoke, she seemed to indicate that she's gone onto higher-end hooking, seeing wealthy European clients. That might not be such a bad thing for Brazil. If anything can advance the country's status on the world stage, it's Lisa and her unique gift for international diplomacy.

CHAPTER EIGHT

Rio Express

THE DIFFERENCE BETWEEN IAN AND ME WAS THAT I DIDN'T SIT around and mope when I got hungry for Rio. Instead, I came up with harebrained schemes to get myself back there. One of my aborted ideas involved launching a website for gringos filled with reviews of Rio's hookers: "GarotaGuide.com. Get the Best Bangs for Your Bucks in Rio. Copacabana's Hottest Girls Reviewed and Rated for Your Convenience."

As I explained in a proposal I emailed to some mongers I knew who had a soft spot for Brazil, the site would invite mongers to rate pros on everything from looks and hygiene to ability in bed to "overall bang for the buck."

The kicker, though, which would have allowed us to stand apart from other monger websites like ISG and WSG would be an online "Garota Tracking System" where we'd input the latest sightings of specific girls. "Click the girl's name and a mock GPS screen shows, for example, her shifting her base of operations from Help to Solarium to Centaurus, etc."

One friend told me to add to the review criteria "blow job ability and, also, how fast she wants to leave your apartment to get back to work."

Another friend wrote back: "Seriously folks, that is the kind of job I am looking for. What a great job that would be. A Brazilian Programa Rater. I would let them all know that I was the U.S. rater, and that if they didn't swallow, I'd give them a rotten review."

Sort of like Hotels.com reviewers.

Sometimes I go even further off the deep end. Especially when I take Triazolam, the generic version of the sleeping pill Halcion. In the period between ingesting the pills and zonking out (usually a half hour), I've sent emails I don't remember writing (including an "advice column" to porn actress Shy Love which I'll tell you about later), consumed food I don't remember eating, and relieved myself to porn I don't remember seeing. Once, I created this webpage, which I thankfully never attempted to seriously promote:

Help Monger Joe Get Laid! Support Monger Joe's World Sex Tour!

I'm Monger Joe. Just your typical average Joe. But I have a dream. A glorious dream. To fuck as many of the world's hottest babes as possible. And you can help it come true. How?

Well, if I wasn't so average, maybe I could just walk into a bar and score with gorgeous girls on a regular basis. But I'm more George Costanza than George Clooney. And I drive a broken-down Buick. So most hot chicks don't exactly wet their panties at the sight of me.

But that's OK, because I've become a huge fan of "pay-for-play"—i.e., "pussy-for-pay," "working girls."

You get the point.

So now I'm a full-fledged monger. A sex tourist who's journeyed to Rio de Janeiro nearly a dozen times since 2003, as well as to Costa Rica and the Dominican Republic a few times. There was even one occasion where I found myself wearing a Mexican wrestling mask while fucking two of the hottest chicks in porn.

Let's make this a banner year for Monger Joe. Your help will let me fuck hundreds of the world's hottest hookers. (Only in places where prostitution is legal, and only with prostitutes of legal age. I'm not a fuckin' pedophile, and I don't go for girls in pigtails and braces or sucking on a lollipop with that stupid "look at me I just sprouted my first pube" look.)

Help me live the dream. For all of us! Remember: I'm doing it as much for you as for me. My dick is your dick. (So to speak.)

Give what you can, anything from $1 to $1 million. In return, you'll get the following items as a precious memento of Monger Joe's World Sex Tour:

For $10, I'll send you an mp3 of a whore screaming your name as I fuck her ($9 or less gets you an mp3 of me screaming your name).

For $20, autographed panties with an inscribed message from a ho—"To the best fuck I ever had." ($2 or less, you're welcome to a pair of my underwear with pee stains still visible.)

For $1, a used condom (depending on local laws regarding shipments of potentially biohazardous materials) from my sex tour. Monger Joe's a big believer in safe sex. (If for some reason you don't want the condom, I won't send it.)

Unfortunately, your gift is NOT tax deductible. Strange as it seems, the IRS doesn't consider helping a guy get laid a charitable endeavor. Here's a rough idea of how much I need to plug those luscious luv-holes that I'll encounter in Rio and other sizzling sex markets:

Airfare: $800

Hotel: $600

Cialis: $100 (This little magic pill is sold over-the-counter in Brazil. 10 pills at about $10 a pop should give my battering ram all the juice it needs.)

Pussy: $7,500 (The better Brazilian *putas* charge $100-$150. On this budget, I should be able to nail at least 50 grade-A whores.)

Food, drink, etc: $1,500 (Monger Joe can't fuck all the time!)

TOTAL: $10,500

CHAPTER NINE

Czech Mates

THE FALL OF COMMUNISM IN EASTERN EUROPE, ONE OF GLOBAL-ization's watershed moments, has spurred the sex trade there. The Czech Republic, at the crossroads of Eastern and Western Europe, is now a hub for sex tourism.

Human trafficking helps to feed the demand for sex workers, but it is unclear to what extent. According to University of Rhode Island Professor Donna Hughes, a leading researcher on trafficking, the Czech "sex trade has gone [from 1994 to 2004] from being almost nonexistent to a hundred-million dollar moneymaking industry for organized-crime networks and collaborating corrupt officials. The women and children who are used for the sex acts get to keep little of the money; in fact, most of them are victims of sex trafficking."

In its 2007 Country Reports on Human Rights Practices, the U.S. State Department wrote that Czech authorities investigated twenty trafficking cases in 2007. "Five offenders were prosecuted and four convicted, one of whom received a suspended sentence. Through June of 2007 police conducted thirty-nine investigations of pimping. The government often utilizes other criminal statutes to prosecute traffickers, making an accurate estimate of the number of actual trafficking cases difficult to ascertain. Fifty-five perpetrators were prosecuted, leading to thirty-four convictions, twenty-eight of which resulted in suspended sentences."

Beyond the issue of trafficking, the Czech flesh trade overall operates in a legal gray zone, and the sexy city of Prague is known as Europe's stag party capital. Among the brothels is one of the world's most innovative pleasure palaces, Big Sister, which may be the ultimate marriage of sex tourism and technology. Sex at the brothel is free—subsidized by subscribers to Big Sister's website—as long as patrons agree to live webcasts of their encounters with prostitutes.

The brothel, whose name is more of a twist on the *Big Brother* TV series than Orwell, pitches its website as an erotic reality show.

"Imagine the pleasure of witnessing the actions of a live working 'brothel' . . . you will be able to view the erotic, the unpredictable, the funny and the sad. Everything is 100% live and unrehearsed . . . . You can watch the girls meeting guests. Watch them perform a striptease, lesbian or an auto-erotic show. . . . Watch them service the guests within the exotic bedrooms of the house. EVERYTHING is on camera. . . . [This] unique project will show you the ups and downs of the oldest profession in the world."

Big Sister's "exotic bedrooms" include an all-white "Heaven"; a dungeon ("Hell"); an Arabian Nights–themed harem room; and an igloo with a stuffed polar bear. There's also an Alpine room where you have to climb a small mountain to get into bed.

The brothel got some interesting publicity when scenes for *Hostel: Part II*, the sequel to every monger's worst nightmare, were shot there. Big Sister has also been covered by *Bloomberg News* ("Free Sex at Prague Brothel Tests Taboo as Reality Romps Hit Web," in January of 2008).

The club features girls from the Czech Republic, Ukraine, the Caribbean, and Brazil. Obviously, with guests' escapades being broadcast over the Internet, it's not for the fainthearted.

A post from "Caiguy" on ISG wonders about the political consequences of "actually getting busted" by your spouse, kids, "boss, or press who found you online." Caiguy says he plans to run someday for the U.S. Senate, "and after the Larry Craig thing, you can't be too careful about your mongering!"

"Mandrake" stresses that just one video of Caiguy can remain in circulation forever. If he's serious about running for public office, "then I would advice [sic] you to stay away."

"Wan King," another poster on ISG, responded to my request for feedback on Big Sister for my book by telling me that Big Sister sucks. While the concept is a good one, apparently mongers aren't allowed to lick pussy or ass. Blow jobs require condoms. Even so, "Wan King" has been to Big Sister five times. Can't be that bad, I guess.

Besides hooking up with prostitutes in the lounge or on the dance floor, you can also review the available talent on one of the club's computers, which are updated daily. From Big Sister's perspective, the key is to find someone you have good chemistry with, or your online sexcast will suck.

"Viscount007" reports on ISG that Big Sister is conveniently located. Apparently, it is one of the easiest clubs to get to despite being on the far side of the Vltava river—just across from the Metro station, you're greeted on entry to Big Sister by a gentleman who explains everything (as if people going there didn't know already).

Then there are six pages of legal documents to sign. Every last detail is in the contact—but for "free" sex, most men seem more than willing to sign on the dotted line.

Then you can start to unwind. There's a bar on the ground floor, and every quarter of an hour a girl does a sexy pole dance, and every hour that girl does a strip tease. Not exactly the place to go for thrills. The girls are usually all busy—keeping the live feed going for their Internet fans.

Viscount suggests going to Big Sister one night just to figure out which girls you like at the computer. Be prepared to dispense with the freebie altogether and pay for the girl you want. When Viscount posted this report in July 2007, he noted the cost as around the equivalent of $140 for an hour. You get plenty for your money, he feels—hot women, a great atmosphere, and it's "only a little more expensive than many *Privats*," the term for private apartments where working girls service clients.

Oh, the Golden City. I can only imagine the pleasures I have yet to discover there—pleasures that could be broadcast by Big Sister all over the Internet. Luckily, modesty has never been one of my strong suits.

CHAPTER TEN

Is That a Wiener Schnitzel in Your Lederhosen? Or Are You Just Happy to See Me?

IF YOU'RE READING THIS (AND HAVE PAID FOR THE PRIVILEGE), I should be that much closer to affording my first trip to Europe's most salacious playground: Germany. I hadn't realized how liberated the Teutonic libido had become until I discovered a poster on ISG who calls himself "Jackyo." He's filed nearly 2,300 posts on ISG detailing his excursions from home in "puritanical" New England to Germany and its sex clubs, where he estimates he's slept with close to four hundred prostitutes.

We spoke at length on the phone about his activities abroad.

"I've done lots of crazy things which I shouldn't have done," he says. "But I'm still around so thank goodness." Like mongering itself, Jackyo says that "posting is habit forming."

Jackyo is in his early fifties and has never been married. He notes that regular German women "have no clue as to what they're up against" with all this information available online. His point could apply equally to women—wives, girlfriends—across the globe. "They think all is fine and dandy and they can continue the way they

117

are," he says. "But when you go to Germany and you just experience what services are offered and how beautiful the women are and that kind of thing . . . it's kind of a backlash against feminism in a way."

Jackyo describes himself as "average looking. I wear glasses, have gray hair, an average build. One might think I look nerdy." He calls German sex clubs "one of the few places where you can just be yourself and do what you want. You can look at women and they expect you to look at them. That's part of the deal. That's really what they're there for, to put themselves on display for you. There's no inhibitions, no nothing."

In Germany, going to brothels "is a very middle-class kind of thing to do," says Jackyo, who describes his career as "publishing support," declining to get more specific. "It's not just the higher end of society that goes and does this. Everybody does it. You meet people from all walks of life."

Jackyo's enthusiasm for Deutschland's sex scene is well grounded in the country's history. In the middle ages, the Holy Roman Emperor Sigismund organized the Council of Constance, a gathering of Catholic religious leaders, to resolve the Great Schism in which rivals claimed to be pope. A reported 1,500 prostitutes flooded the city of Konstanz in Germany's southwest corner to serve the secular needs of the attendees. This happy mingling of clergy and courtesans was commemorated in 1993 with the Imperia, a twenty-seven-foot-high statue overlooking the city's harbor. The controversial sculpture, named after a legendary Italian prostitute, shows her holding in each hand tiny versions of the emperor and the Council's choice for Pope, Martin V.

"Since the early Renaissance, the attitude toward commercial sex in the German-speaking lands has always been more relaxed than elsewhere on the continent," notes the *London Telegraph*. German writers in the fifteenth century affectionately referred to prostitutes, who tended to flock around cathedrals, as "swallows." Still, working girls were compelled to identify themselves by wearing red berets or green sashes.

According to the *Telegraph*, "sometimes the authorities got even more involved, and ended up managing or even establishing 'municipal' bordellos of their own. In one Germanic city in 1521 the state went the whole hog: 'swallows' were shifted en masse to the outer suburbs, where special villas were erected for them at taxpayers' expense."

Today, about 400,000 people work in Germany's sex trade. The country legalized its thriving flesh industry in 2002, guaranteeing prostitutes the same rights as other workers, including health insurance. For their part, prostitutes must register with the authorities and pay taxes.

Official acceptance of prostitution sometimes manifests itself in quirky ways. When Germany prepared to host the 2006 World Cup, some of the host cities built wooden drive-in huts, or "action boxes," equipped with condom machines and snack bars. The huts were designed to handle the boom in the sex trade that was expected to accompany the World Cup, and keep people from consummating their business out in the open.

The World Cup also generated darker fears about the sex trade. Major news outlets dutifully repeated the predictions of some trafficking experts that as many as forty thousand women from

Eastern Europe, Latin America, and Asia would be forced to work as prostitutes in Germany during the games. Ultimately, the German police only found five cases of trafficking linked to the World Cup.

This is not to say that trafficking doesn't exist in Germany. According to the U.S. Department of State's 2008 "Trafficking in Persons Report," German authorities identified 775 sex-trafficking victims in 2006, the last year for which data was available.

"I'd like to think [all the girls in the brothels he visits] are making informed decisions, that they know what they're up to, that they're not being trafficked," Jackyo says. But he understands that might be wishful thinking.

As a way of screening out possible trafficking victims, he looks for girls who speak German. "If she speaks it well, even if she's foreign, she's [probably] been in Germany for a couple of years," he says, noting that a prostitute "who doesn't speak German at all or speaks it very poorly" is more likely to be there against her will. "But women like that I can't communicate with anyway," he says. "So one of my criteria is that I am able to communicate with her."

Jackyo adds that the further a prostitute is from home, the greater the chances that she's a victim of traffickers. How, he wonders, "does a Ukrainian woman, for example, who speaks no German, ever figure out how to get to a club and work there? What would ever possess her to decide that this is a career choice? That does bother me. If she's communicative, if she can express herself, I worry about it less. . . . It's the quiet ones who sit there with nothing to say that make you wonder."

Later, he emails me the link for a website, www.stop-forced-prostitution.de, that shows how to recognize if a sex worker's been trafficked. Anyone who's setting out on a mongering trip should familiarize himself with the site and its common-sense recommendations. These include asking yourself questions like these: Does the woman seem intimidated or disoriented? Excessively exhausted or fatigued? Does she show signs of maltreatment? Is she escorted by a third party? The site also addresses what to do if you notice any of these red flags.

* * * *

For Jackyo, Germany is the ultimate mongering spot. "People have this impression that if you want sex in Europe you go to France." But, "France is terrible for this," he says, recalling his travels there in recent years. "It's really really bad. . . . French women are a pain in the ass, stuck up. I don't know what it is. They're all very tense and slightly neurotic, that kind of thing. . . . They're nice to look at, though. . . . You go to Germany, the woman are just like, 'Hey, you know, it's sex, people do it, everybody does it.' You don't hide these things, you just do it. . . . That's the way it should be. Just that mentality is so different."

Amsterdam's notorious red light district also doesn't cut it for him. Those beckoning women in the window, he says, are all in *upsell mode* where everything beyond basic sex costs extra. Once she gets you in the room and she knows she's got your libido on a string, she'll hit you up for more cash, telling you "'Oh, you can't touch that. . . . We can't change positions.' It just kills the mood," he says.

Apparently, a lot of Dutch men feel the same. Jackyo often meets them in German sex clubs near the Dutch border. "The Dutch know a good deal when they see it," he says.

In Germany itself, Jackyo stays off the beaten track. He considers Hamburg's sex-drenched Reeperbahn, also known as the "Genital Zone," another tourist trap, filled with clip joints. In many of the strip clubs, the dancers, he notes, "are available for pick-up." But when you try to hammer out a deal, she'll say, "Get me a bottle of champagne and we can talk about what we're going to do next."

Bait and switch is *verboten* in the types of German brothels—*partytreffs* and *FKKs*—that Jackyo frequents. These clubs draw patrons who "don't like surprises in pricing," he says. "They like predictability and I like that, too. I don't like this idea of negotiating everything. . . . For me that's just not the way to go."

FKK stands for *frei koerper kultur*, or "free body culture" in English. FKKs originally referred to nudist colonies that didn't necessarily involve sex, especially the paid kind. But in many German brothels, prostitutes and customers walk around nude, or wrapped in towels, and such establishments have taken to calling themselves FKKs. Like Rio's termas, FKKs offer other amenities besides sex, such as saunas, massages, food, and drink. The typical entry fee is around $75, and $130 will get you an hour with a girl. FKK girls are technically considered guests, so they also pay the entry fee, which they can recoup in their first session.

Over the last four or five years, *partytreffs* have emerged as a pay-one-price alternative to FKKs. "Basically, you pay one fee at a partytreff, you go in, you got food and drink, and you can stay as long as you want," says Jackyo. "You have a selection of women and you can have sex as much as you want to, which is amazing. . . . You can spend the whole day and screw and eat and drink and all your needs are taken care of, which just blows the mind."

Of course, a day of constant fucking can be draining. "It's almost as much a test of your endurance" as it is sex, says Jackyo. "It's still an interesting thing to do. But I just don't know if it's really sex. Or what even to call it."

Older partytreffs, such as Dolce Vita in Lower Saxony and Dorsten in North Rhine-Westphalia, charge about $150. Some of the newer ones, like Traumland and PolePosition, both in North Rhine-Westphalia , cost around $225 for the day or $150 for three hours.

A partytreff might get fifty to sixty clients on a regular day, and up to one hundred on weekends with reduced entry fees. Jackyo advises that it's "best not to go" on such days. "The clubs run out of lockers and you have to stuff your valuables and clothes into a plastic bag."

In partytreffs, a girl makes about $15 for everyone that pays an entrance fee. The girls don't have to screw every guy in the place, but they're technically always on the clock, so if they're not in a session, they have to make themselves available.

This take-on-all-comers system seems to run smoothly. In all his visits to partytreffs, Jackyo's only been turned down twice—not surprisingly, in a club he doesn't go to anymore. If a partytreff girl should reject you, don't take it too hard, he advises. "If she didn't like you to begin with, and you insisted on going with her, you'd probably get lousy service anyway." You're better off, he says, saving yourself "some money and some aggravation. There's so many choices of women that you shouldn't sweat it."

Perhaps it's not always personal, either, I tell him, noting that a girl might be exhausted from catering to so many men that day. Jackyo adds that sometimes a girl's waiting for a regular client with whom she's already comfortable. "Why is she going to pick one random guy like me who happens to be wandering by?" he asks. Still, whatever her reasons, Jackyo says that in a well-run partytreff, a hooker could get fired for turning down even one guest.

Jackyo's family is from southern Germany, and he's been visiting that part of the country for years. But as with many mongers, it was the Internet that suggested a new dimension to his trips. In 1998, he began reading about the country's sex clubs on a German-language website. The following year he decided to take the plunge and find out if all the raunchy things he'd been reading were for real.

All it took was a visit to Bernds Sauna Club, an FKK in Hennef, a small town near Cologne, and he was sold. "It's the mother of all clubs," he says, echoing the slogan on Bernds's website, *Mutter aller Clubs.*"

Online men's magazine AskMen.com rates Bernds number six on its list of the world's Top Ten Brothels. The club "is more of a house," says AskMen. It even has a garden where the prostitutes splash around in a kiddy pool.

"Bernds is the one that's been around the longest," says Jackyo. "It's got a cult following." Despite its reputation, not all mongers post glowing reports about Bernds. "Some new guys go there, they write back, 'I don't get it, I just don't get it,'" he notes. Jackyo advises them: "Don't go because you're looking for women who look great."

"You will not find any nines or tens there. But you get good service, and the selection is 'edited'"—management strives to keep a balance of blondes, brunettes, Romanians, Germans, etc., so the girls don't look like clones.

At Bernds and other German sex clubs, "the Berlin Wall coming down is what opened everything up," he says. "Eastern European women have raised the bar. They have a different perspective on things. They're not like Westernized women who demand and expect certain things. They would rather take care of their men and that's the way they're brought up." He adores Polish women. "I'm going to learn Polish eventually. I need to." He tries to pick up the language from girls in the clubs. "It leads to funny conversations where I'm practicing on them," he says. "They're teaching me stuff, and we're screwing at the same time. Or poking, at least."

Bernds tries, he adds, "to provide the best service possible . . . . They're not clock-watchers. You can take as much time as you want. The women there are cool, they're easy to talk to. . . . It's got a service orientation that's just not the same in the large clubs. . . . You can have sex outside if you want, you can have it inside. You can jerk off on the couch if you want to, nobody will bat an eyelash. The best session I had there . . . it wasn't even like real sex was involved. We just sat on the couch and she turned me on like you wouldn't believe. It had nothing to do with any penetration or anything like that. I was just sitting there and I was so excited, I lost it.

"It wasn't even like she was the best-looking woman in the room. It's just she'd looked appealing and I went up to her and we made out on the couch. And the way she hovered about me, and the way she just looked at me like there was nobody else there. I don't know what it was. It was very odd, it was very strange. She just has a way of doing it. It's like minimal contact, but you know you were clicking with her, and that was enough."

Girls at Bernds—and at Babylon, another club near Cologne—are not allowed to aggressively approach customers. "The only way that she can catch your attention is to do something," says Jackyo. "She opens her legs and she starts playing with herself. Who's going to ignore that?"

Some men respond with what he calls the "connect-with-a-gaze-from-far-away-and-cock-your-head" motion. "Before you know it she crosses the room and she's sitting in your lap. . . . I don't have the technique perfected, but I tried it at this one club across a crowded room." Instantly, "there she was" in his lap. "We were like old friends."

I have a similar technique in Rio, I tell him. When I see a cute working girl, I'll play peekaboo with her. If she laughs, then I at least know she has a sense of humor.

Despite his family ties to southern Germany, he finds the sex clubs there too expensive. "People sometimes post about going to southern Germany . . . looking for action," he says—Munich in particular. Jackyo steers them north, where you get more bang for your euro. Also, the south's Catholic conservatism means certain restrictions are in place, like laws against bareback blow jobs.

Ironically, it was under history's most vicious right-winger that conservative views on prostitution were not only ignored, but could actually lead to trouble with Hitler's Gestapo. While the Nazis cracked down on streetwalkers, they *ordered* the establishment of fully regulated brothels in all cities. Various officials had their own reasons for supporting a state-controlled sex trade. The German military considered the availability of prostitutes—certified, of course, as disease-free—vital to the morale of the growing ranks of young recruits who were being molded to conquer Europe. SS chief Heinrich Himmler, the architect of the Nazi police state and the Holocaust, viewed prostitution as a safeguard against homosexuality. As he told SS leaders in a speech in 1937, "Every barred opportunity to get together with girls in the big cities—even if it is for money—will motivate a large contingent to join [in Himmler's words] *the other side.*"

The Nazis also appreciated the value of pillow talk as an espionage tool. According to historian Jacques Delarue, the "depraved taste" of Himmler's deputy, Gestapo boss Reinhard Heydrich, "led him to frequent the dens and red light districts of Berlin." Realizing how much juicy gossip passed from the lips of clients to prostitutes, he created Salon Kitty, a brothel with beautiful hookers handpicked by the Gestapo. The girls "were selected not only for their charm and beauty but also for their intelligence, culture, knowledge of languages, and their 'patriotism.'" The whorehouse was wired from top to bottom with concealed microphones. Salon Kitty drew a "select clientele," including foreign diplomats, who unwittingly gave important information to the Nazis.

The brothel even inspired a 1976 soft-core porn movie of the same name. The director, Tinto Brass, would later go on to cinematic-cluster-fuck immortality with *Caligula.* (Come to think of it, it might have been the depraved emperor, who opened a brothel in his palace, who first exposed the ancient Germans to organized prostitution.)

During the Second World War, the Nazis found additional uses for the sex trade. As Germany filled up with slave labor, mainly from Eastern Europe, the Nazis grew terrified of sexual relations between "sub-humans" and Aryan women. In order to preserve what he felt was the purity of the German blood, Hitler, in fact, ordered the creation of segregated brothels where foreign laborers slept with prostitutes from their own country.

Then, as concentration camps spread across occupied Europe, the Nazis forced between three hundred and four hundred women to become sex workers in brothels in ten concentration camps, including Auschwitz, Dachau, Buchenwald, and Sachsenhausen. According to the *Telegraph* in the UK, the brothels were known as "special barracks," and were "part of a system of incentives intended to boost the productivity of concentration camp slave laborers. These bonuses were not, however, extended to every group of inmates—Jews in particular were excluded."

After the war, the East German secret police, the Stasi, drew inspiration from their Gestapo forebears. The Stasi recruited dozens of prostitutes to obtain information from Western diplomats and businessmen. In East Berlin, the Stasi offered to drop charges against call girls who could get the goods from horny capitalists.

Among the nuggets acquired this way was a report on a British businessman who had a hooker bring a whip to their tryst. Allan Hall writes in the *Times* "The files would be comical were it not for the consequences. [One of the prostitutes] betrayed a ring of would-be escapers from Leipzig who had sought help from Western businessmen. They received long jail terms."

In West Germany during the cold war, foreigners had less to fear from their nocturnal romps. The *Journal of Popular Culture* relates that in German towns with American troops, "bars, massage parlors, brothels ... sprang up" near military bases to boost soldiers' morale. "Prostitutes from across Germany arrived on GI paydays, hotel owners made rooms available by the hour, and young women settled permanently."

Most of the American troops are gone now, but the party still goes on, especially in some of Jackyo's favorite clubs, like FKK Zeus, in the Osnabrueck district in Lower Saxony. "This is easily the best FKK club in this neck of the woods," he says. "The women are nude, there is an open anything-goes atmosphere."

The club typically has ten to fifteen girls, who flirt with customers on the red leather couches in the main parlor. The checkerboard floor adds an elegant touch. Zeus also has an outdoor pool, and a bed in the adjoining garden. "Couch action is offered as well as sex in the open and in doorless rooms," says Jackyo.

Zeus's website (www.fkk-zeus.de) features pictures of the girls, including a pair of uber-breasted blonde and brunette strippers, Darna and Nadja, who perform a live lesbian show. Most of the other girls in the photos have inspirational bodies, too, although their faces are intentionally blurred.

During a visit to Zeus in 2007, Jackyo had a session with Violetta, a twenty-one-year-old platinum blonde from Berlin. "Normally I don't go for this look but she had nice legs, a cute bubble butt, and an amazing smile," says Jackyo. After some brief "couch action," they went into a room with mirrored walls. "I couldn't resist her charms, particularly as she took delight at watching my reactions to her activity," he says. "She could see my face from any angle because of the mirrors."

("Breadman," another ISG poster who was at Zeus with Jackyo, wrote about his own tryst with Thalia, a blonde girl-next-door type with "nice Bs . . . one fine body. Easily a nine in my book." After a bit of small talk on the couch, she pulled off his towel, "grabbed 'little breadman' and said, 'let's see how this tastes.'" Then it was off to the room, where he found her "very responsive . . . with lots of hip movement.")

Zeus scores lower with Jackyo on its culinary offerings. "The only problem with this club is that there is not much to eat at all," he says. "It doesn't quite give you the incentive to spend the whole day."

On the other hand, the day flew by when Jackyo had made his first visit to a partytreff, Dolce Vita, in 2005.

"The concept seemed simple," he reported on ISG after his maiden tour of partytreffs. "Pay once and have as much sex as you want with whoever you wanted to have it with. . . . It seemed almost too good to be true [but] the partytreff scene is for real and it is a great alternative to the pay-per-session clubs."

Jackyo was one of the first mongers to post about partytreffs on ISG. It gave him instant credibility, inspiring others to explore the emerging partytreff scene. Sometimes, he'd muse about clubs that he hadn't been to yet, prompting fellow mongers to try out these places and report back.

Clearly, there's a real hunger for this kind of information. "It's a primal thing, basic instinct," I tell Jackyo. "Men don't really know details. They'll see something on TV about Amsterdam's red light district, but don't really know much. They'll hear whispers, but that's it. The Internet has opened a whole new world for mongers, for better or worse."

Dolce Vita has a lounge, as well as private rooms. The club also has a sauna, heated pool, and a large-screen TV. (This may come as a shock, but no one can fuck all day without an occasional diversion.)

There were eight women at Dolce Vita during Jackyo's first visit: "a thin bleached Polish blonde with boots, a medium-sized nicely shaped German blonde from the Ruhrpott, a Russian blonde with an amazing body—nice, firm tits—a tall Slovakian brunette who was very sweet, a very well formed raven-haired Turkish woman, a small Polish blonde who spoke no German or English at all, another petite Polish blonde with aggressive tattoos (she was just insatiable), then a Polish brunette."

Jackyo says all the women were "nice, accommodating, willing to make some small talk." The sign behind the bar underscored their attitude: *Wer will ficken, muss freundlich sein*—"Whoever wants to fuck must be friendly."

"If one of them saw you sitting in the couch area and you hadn't met yet, she would come up to you and sit to talk," he says. "Before you knew it, you were engaged in some heavy petting or she would go down on you. You then had the option of doing it right there . . . or going back to one of the rooms. Only the rooms downstairs offered any privacy though and sex out in the open was more the norm rather than the exception."

Dolce Vita, he says, is "not for the fainthearted or extra prudish because you will more likely than not have sex in public." Jackyo describes huge gang bangs "every hour on the hour. . . . They just make sure everybody gets satisfied, one way or the other. If there was nothing going on and just groups of guys and girls hanging out, the women would suggest a group activity," says Jackyo. "The women would all find a partner and the whole group would do it right there on the spot. If there was a surplus of women, two of them would do one dude. Once, they dragged the whole lot of us into the small hut in the back with the large mattress. I was just sitting off to one corner watching the activities when one of the small Polish blondes saw me by myself and crawled over to me to make sure I had something to do. Now you understand why I went back a second time."

Jackyo conveys a surreal scene of how men would sit around after orgies "totally drained." Nude women would float from customer to customer, still pitching their services: "You want some? You want some? You want some?" A typical response: "No. I just can't get it up anymore."

Of course, for some of the hookers at Dolce Vita, that's the whole point: to wear the men out so that the girls can sit around and relax. Jackyo's gotten gentle flack during sessions where he didn't come. "I can't say it's because they weren't good enough or anything like that," he says. "I just go, 'Well, maybe a little later.' So it kind of thwarts their plan, which is to make you come as quickly as possible, so they don't have to work as hard. And if I keep thwarting the plan then they keep wondering why, what went wrong, so I've learned to fake it—'Ooh. Ooh. I'm coming, I'm coming.' Then, of course, I don't let them grab the condom and check it." He adds that some of the girls "are so well-lubed, I can't get a grip. You know what I mean? Slippery vaginas. . . . There's no friction."

He asks me if he's "the only [man] facing this problem" of having to fake it. "Not at all," I reassure him. I've had similar experiences in Rio where I couldn't come. Juliana would take especial umbrage at what she considered an insult to her erotic talents. Like Jackyo, I've tried to fake it, too, and discard the condom before my partner could scrutinize it.

Condom inspections are less of a concern at Partytreff Mettmann, in North Rhine-Westphalia near Düsseldorf. "The girls don't even turn around," says Jackyo, who's been there about a half-dozen times. "You just find an open hole, you screw it. . . . It's an acquired taste. Not everybody is comfortable in a club like that."

Overall, Jackyo believes that FKKs hire better-looking women than partytreffs. "There are trade-offs," he says. At partytreffs, "you can't expect you're going to have model-type women all the time." Also, he notes, "the sex may be mechanical. . . . But you poke and you poke and you go, 'Okay, that was nice.' And you break away from her and you pick another one and you do the same thing. You know, it's conversation with poking. Is it really sex? I don't know if it's sex anymore. I'm beyond the point of thinking that it is. Usually it's out in the open and guys walk by. That's just totally normal."

Perhaps the greatest appeal of partytreffs to Jackyo is that many of the workers are "semi-pros," among them college girls looking to make extra money. "When she meets her financial objective, she disappears," he says. "She doesn't need to do this. She figures if she's going to have sex anyway, then she may as well have it and make some money doing it. That's the kind of woman, when you find somebody like that, it's a treat. It's like 'whoa!' She's cool. Because she's not like a pro."

"I'm not looking strictly for an orgasm each time I go [to a sex club]," says Jackyo. "It's all part of the whole human interaction thing. I don't think you can separate one from the other. It's really about making connection, it's learning about other people, other places, just as much as it is finding that chick who really turns you on and who you can never forget."

Jackyo goes to Germany two or three times a year, and he knows that this kind of woman might be out of the business by the time he returns. "When I meet a chick like that, I spend multiple sessions with her," he says. "I only need to find one chick like that in a club, then I'm happy."

He recalls one girl at a club who told him she was in law school and just wanted to cover some bills. "So what are the chances I'm going to see you when I come back in three months?" he asked her. "Zero," she replied. Jackyo made sure to have three sessions with her that day.

The semi-pros tend not to be "dumb as a doorknob" or "peasant chicks from Romania who'd be feeding chickens if they weren't doing this," he says. "What do I have in common with a chick like that? You meet a middle-class woman from Germany and you know where she's coming from. She's into the same popular culture things as you are, you have an idea what she's thinking. You can at least converse on some level. But meet some chick who's been, like, tending goats, and there's just no way you're going to have any kind of conversation."

I tell Jackyo that many of the working girls I've met in Brazil also have a middle-class normalcy about them: "They go to college, they work in an office during the day, and they're moonlighting as prostitutes to make ends meet. Their regular jobs just don't pay enough."

The GFE, he says, "is what I look for more than anything. I've been with women who looked terrific but they were just duds. There's nothing there. She's there physically but she's just not there." New mongers, he says, probably don't even recognize the signs. "They don't follow the body language, they don't look at their eyes and figure out if she's just going through the motions."

Despite the extraordinary GFEs I've had in Latin America, I tell Jackyo that I've encountered my share of prostitutes who are all business. The first words out of their mouth are "Do you want company tonight?" I don't mind the directness, but it has to be combined with seductiveness. If she knows how to touch you or tease you right off the bat, she can trigger the fantasy that she's not just interested in money.

"Body language matters a lot," Jackyo says. "I like to think that I'm not influenced so much by the way she looks but by her service. But guess what. In some instances, that rule just gets thrown out the window. I'm looking at her and I go, 'Man, I've got to have this one.'"

He also longs for the post-coital sessions that used to be routinely held at Babylon, where the girls would spend time with you after sex. "If it wasn't busy, you'd just sit, you'd cuddle," he says. "She didn't charge you more. It was just two people hanging out and talking, that's all."

Even today, the girls at Babylon can still sit with you when you're done, but it's their call. "If you're entertaining, if you're a nice person to hang out with, she will," says Jackyo.

"Professionals or not, they're still human," I chime in. "They still respond to the laws of attraction or chemistry, or comfort with someone."

There are times, however, when a bitch is just what the doctor ordered. "Sometimes I'm in the mood for a bitchy or moody ice queen," says Jackyo. "Sometimes I just would rather she didn't have anything to say at all. . . . I just want to get it over with and move on and don't really want to have any kind of interaction with her."

In Brazilian brothels, it's common for the girls to give clients their phone numbers, and meet them for sex outside of work. Jackyo's never done this with a German sex worker. A friend of his tried it once, and the club banned him. Brazilian clubs frown upon it too, I tell him. The trick, of course, is to do it discreetly, out of sight of the club's managers.

At the very least, Jackyo struck me as the kind of guy who'd stay in friendly contact with some of the girls, perhaps through email. "I've never gotten to that point," he says. One girl he's particularly fond of at Bernds "keeps her private life very separate. I'll say things like 'Why don't you come and visit me? I'll send you a plane ticket.' She'll go 'My boyfriend would not like that. He would not approve of this happening.'"

I tell him that Brazilian girls seem to go out of their way to prove that they don't have boyfriends or husbands. Which I always find peculiar. Half of them, at least, have to be full of shit because they're too hot, they're too sexual, to not have boyfriends when they're not working. It's got to be part of their game, part of their spiel, so they can convince you that there's nothing in the way of a real GFE.

Jackyo has some of his most intense GFEs with a pro he sees regularly in the U.S. He likens her to a geisha. She not only cooks for him, but they exchange recipes. "She says 'you should try this, try that,'" says Jackyo. "Then we have sex." She's also well read, "an interesting person to talk to."

With almost four hundred hookers under his belt ("I have a list actually," he tells me. "Not that I'm proud of that number, but I do have a list somewhere"), he's still not sure what all that mongering adds up to.

"I kind of just ask myself philosophical questions," he says. "What am I getting out of this, what am I learning out of this? Why do they call it 'carnal knowledge'? What do I know about these women when I'm done with my 'poking sessions'? Nothing really. I know nothing. There's no knowledge there. . . . Not that I'm going to give it up anytime soon. But it does make you ask those questions."

"Plenty of guys find themselves asking why they don't feel complete after years of marriage," I remind him. Does that mean their marriages are meaningless? Such questions are not inherent in the specific activity (marriage, mongering, etc.); it's the human mind at work, doing what it does instinctively, which is to ask: What the hell's going on here? What am I doing? Everyone asks these things, regardless of their life's circumstances.

After all his sexcapades, would it be harder for Jackyo to have a relationship with a non-pro? Jackyo was dating somebody for a few months at the beginning of 2008. He says that mongering has not given him unrealistic expectations. "Am I 'spoiled' about it? I don't know," he says. "I mean I don't push civilian women, I don't make them do things that I've had [prostitutes] do with me. . . . My expectation is that they're not going to do certain things and they don't. If they do it, then quite simply I'm pleasantly surprised. If they don't, then that's fine too."

Jackyo acknowledges, however, that his experiences in Germany would make it harder for him to stay monogamous. "That is the biggest problem," he says. "It's like, man, am I stuck with this chick for the next—who knows how many years? Am I going to wake up every morning and see the same thing and do the same thing every evening?"

Clearly, there are advantages to being in a committed relationship, including, of course, free sex. One of the trade-offs, though, is that you lose the freedom to come and go as you please. With a pro, "it's clean, it's easy, and you don't have the strings attached after the fact," says Jackyo. "There's something to be said for that. You know, maybe it does turn out cheaper in the end that way. You're not sneaking around, trying to get away from somebody. I like women, I just like to do it on my own terms. I don't want to end up in a situation where they're calling the shots."

A monger's life is not for everyone. But in the pleasure parlors of Germany, Jackyo seems to have found his niche.

CHAPTER ELEVEN

The Shy Love Letter

AMONG THE WACKIEST THINGS I'VE DONE TO IMPRESS A PORN star was emailing an advice column to Latina actress Shy Love. I sent it in response to an article she'd penned for *Rock Confidential* magazine on her search for true love. In my defense, I wrote it on one of my Triazolam-fueled flights of fancy and was mortified to see it the next morning in my sent folder. Ironically, she's not even one of my favorites, though she does have a cute overbite.

> To: Shy Love
> From: Rio Joe
> Subject: *Rock Confidential*: Love Looking For Lov

> Dear Shy,
> I loved your latest column. You address so many fundamental issues that have bewildered lovers since the beginning of time.
> As you wrote: "I'm more of a softy at heart who is searching for someone to talk to and cuddle with. If I could describe

the love I would try and use lyrics of love songs and even the sonnets of Shakespeare and it would be impossible, because the love that I long for is real, unconditional, everlasting and indescribable. To me the love is living life like it's an adventure and enjoying every special moment. Love is worth fighting for, risking everything for, and the trouble is, if you don't risk everything, you risk even more."

So true! Those who refuse to take risks often find that life throws even more risks their way, which they're usually unprepared for.

"In my past I have always looked for a partner to make me feel worthwhile, to make me feel happy, to rescue me from a boring unhappy life," you wrote. "But what I did not understand is that I should not have been seeking someone to make me feel complete or whole, what I should have done is make myself happy because these are needs that are never going to be met by anyone other than myself."

Essentially what you want is an "equal partner" whose main concern is building a life with you by allowing you both to explore your careers and other major interests, then finding true love at the intersection of both your and his needs, interests and accomplishments.

"The most important thing for me to be in a relationship is to find a man that can give me mutual respect."

When the two of you have achieved the things that are uniquely important to each of you as individuals, then you can share your respective accomplishments in order to create a solid foundation for a life together. But it's vital that each of you have time to grow as individuals, so that you can both channel your personal successes into a healthy, happy relationship.

Stranger things have happened, but I think I'd be ideal for you. I'm based in New York, though, which might be a bit of an obstacle. But I'm sure we can put our heads together and figure out something, if you're interested in talking more.

Best wishes,

Joe Diamond

www.riojoe.com

I signed off with a list of my porn "credentials," hoping to signal to her that I wasn't just some obsessed fan. (No, I was just some wacko porn journalist.)

Writer:

1) Playboy TV's *69 Sexy Things To Do Before You Die*

2) *Hustler* magazine

3) *Maxim*

4) XBIZ

5) Other outstanding literary journals, including *Screw, Club, Oui,* and *Busty Beauties.*

Author of upcoming book on sex tourism, *Around the World in 80 Lays.*

Blog: "Sex Tourism/Sex Travel—Adventures of an Average Joe" http://riojoe.com/rjblog

If she ever responds to me, and takes me up on my offer to get together, she might be able to save me a fortune on future excursions to Brazil and other foreign flesh markets. Of course, I have plenty of women to keep myself occupied while I entertain that fantasy.

CHAPTER TWELVE

I Am the Mask

I ENCOUNTERED GOOD LUCK IN MY QUEST FOR A PORN STAR EXPER-ience (PSE) when I got involved with a website (later a video series) that featured anonymous guys in wacky Mexican wrestling masks—everything from a lizard head to a jack-o'-lantern—doing very nasty things with porn chicks. BeTheMask.com picked a different member each month to appear on the site, a genius-level marketing tactic which helped drive paid subscriptions through the roof.

I was offered the February of 2004 slot. It was not a good time for me, love-wise. I had another trip to Brazil planned for later that month, but I was striking out a lot at home. One night in a Manhattan bar, all it took was a simple hello to a cute blonde to get a drink tossed in my face. The next night I tried to talk to a nubile thing in a tight sweater. Grabbing her friend, she said, "I'm a lesbian. I don't talk to guys." As I'd witnessed her swapping spit with three guys in the last hour, I knew what she really meant was, "I don't talk to guys *like you.*"

It's like that joke: What's the difference between a slut and a bitch? A slut fucks everybody. A bitch fucks everybody but you.

That wasn't the first time I've heard the "I'm a lesbian" line. Last year, I was having a pretty decent conversation with a girl at a club in New York when her friend interrupted with, "Don't talk to her. She's mine." Drunk and in no mood for games, I responded, "She's too cute to be with you." The girl clocked me.

BeTheMask offered me redemption. I could go from loser to red-hot lover of sex starlets instantly. I informed the webmaster, Scott, that I would gladly serve as the next Mask. He seemed oddly relieved. It wasn't always easy, he explained, to get fans, even when hidden behind a cowl, to agree to perform on camera. I could see their point, but I was too pumped up on frustration and bravado to weasel out.

After arranging things with Scott, I scoured BeTheMask.com to see their available talent. After all, they were letting me choose my own partner. But which one? Scott's girlfriend at the time was Welsh sex kitten Kelle Marie, a former *Penthouse* model. She would have made for a nice choice, but Scott said she was "off-limits to other guys."

With Kelle out of the mix, I zeroed my sights in on Brittney Skye, a tanned blonde with a great boob job who resembled a younger, foxier Jenna Jameson.

As the reality of what awaited me set in, my anxiety grew, and I nearly called Scott to back out. I was flabby, pasty, and modestly equipped. How would I measure up in Ms. Skye's eyes? How would it look on video? Could I really stay hard when surrounded by a camera crew? I wanted my first Porn Star Experience to be a good one.

"Swinger," a contributor to online slang bible Urban Dictionary, defines the PSE as a notch above a Girlfriend Experience. Another contributor, "AdriannaGFE," goes further, calling it an encounter with a partner who's bent on pleasing you with certain porn-like characteristics, like talking dirty and "CIM (cum in mouth)."

There's no doubt in my mind why I was drawn to porn journalism. I wanted to get as close to porn chicks as possible, always hoping for a GFE or PSE with a PS. Now was my chance.

I booked the flight and decided to find out just how it felt to "be the mask." Then I called my doctor for my first taste of Viagra.

I had two weeks to prepare for my porn debut. It wasn't quite like training to fight the champ, but it was still a major challenge for me. My nervous system was on overload. I started hitting the gym, hoping to streamline my gut and at least firm up my pectorals a bit. Not that they could be (nor would I want them to be) any match for Brittney's silicone sensations.

I was too scared of skin cancer to use a tanning bed. But then I remembered an episode of *Friends* I had seen in which David Schwimmer's character Ross got a spray-on tan. Mystic Tan, the product's manufacturer, had a booth near my gym. It's as easy as taking a shower. You just turn after so many seconds to ensure an even tan. I was determined to do better than Ross, who of course bungled it by turning too late and kept doing it over until he looked like a Baked Alaska.

I didn't want to take any chances. I got my Mystic Tan a week before my trip to leave time for any potential mistakes to wear off. By the next morning, though, once the color settled in, I was thrilled. I looked like I'd been to Hawaii.

The next challenge involved my stamina. My fear was that I'd take one look at Brittney and explode on contact. Viagra might stiffen you up, but it doesn't give you greater control. I was no long-distance runner, and I knew Brittney deserved better than my typical three minutes. So I decided to build self-discipline by practicing to her flicks.

I practiced every day to Brittney classics like *Lesbian Hooter Party, Panty Paradise*, and *Decadent Divas 22*. As the first title suggests, these were all videos of Brittney doing other girls, which I loved. The only porn I like is lesbian porn. Why would I want to fantasize to other guys picking up hot chicks and screwing them? That's what happened to me in real life.

I practiced assiduously several times a day, steadily building control. Baby oil can be dangerous, though. Everything gets slicked up, even the bottle. During one particularly intense self-love session, the container slipped from my grip as I was pouring and smashed into my testicles. I felt like Mel Gibson getting eviscerated at the end of *Braveheart*. My sack swelled up like a grapefruit. Would Brittney be worth it? I'd soon find out.

Scott and Kelle Marie picked me up at the airport in Los Angeles. Our first stop was AIM Healthcare, the adult industry's very own STD testing center. Just like the pros, I was tested for the big four— HIV, chlamydia, gonorrhea, and syphilis. Now I really felt like a porn stud. Results typically took about a day. I'd been tested before, but I was still relieved to learn that my adventures in Brazil (and the Dominican Republic at the end of 2003) hadn't left me with any nasty surprises, and my clean bill of health guaranteed me smooth sailing into the Bay of Brittney.

She arrived at Scott's studio the morning of the shoot for makeup. Even in sweats, her fun bags made quite an impression. I introduced myself by telling her that her videos had given me "great pleasure."

How much Viagra was I supposed to take? Twenty-five or a hundred milligrams? I chose the latter. Almost immediately, my head felt like it was going to float off my neck, like I'd just smoked an entire field of marijuana. This is probably because all the blood had left my brain and rushed to my penis. You could have shoved me into Rosie O'Donnell's snatch and I'd still have been as hard as a redwood.

I got to choose Brittney's outfit, a see-through pink top, and my mask, a camouflage-patterned hood from Scott's collection that made me look like GI Joe gone postal.

Scott had wanted me to fuck Brittney condomless, but that little latex "mask" gave me an even greater sense of security than the one covering my face.

We started with a photo session, keeping perfectly still as Scott directed us through a dozen positions. She reared up and posed doggy-style on my dick, then reverse cowgirl, then me on top. That was torture, trying to keep still with my prick bopping around inside of Brittney. I was aching to make some friction.

Finally came the video shoot. I was more than happy to let Brittney take the lead, as she was no mannequin. Everything she did was mind-blowing: riding me, nibbling me, thrusting her freshly douched joy hole in my face, smothering my manhood between her breasts. She oozed lust. Her eyes were blazing, her lips pouty, wet, and slightly parted, always ready to chomp on any part of my anatomy within striking distance.

Scott encouraged me to stick it in Brittney's ass (hey, what's a porn scene without some assplay?), but—pun intended—I've always been a bit too anal (as in neat-freakish) to travel that road. Still, if Brittney had commanded me to fuck her ass in that smoky voice of hers, I admit I might have caved.

Scott wanted around twenty minutes of footage and I almost made it, popping my cork in about fourteen minutes. For a first-timer, I was satisfied with my performance, even a bit proud I'd held out that long.

Of course, the thought nagged at me that all this had meant nothing to Brittney. (My worst fears would be reinforced at the adult video convention the following January, when I bumped into Brittney and she seemed to have no idea who I was.) She had been paid to do a scene in which I happened to be the costar. I was basically a prop, the porn equivalent of a stripper's pole. But it was still awesome. There should be a law that says every guy gets to boink a porn star at least once in his life. I'd had my first PSE and I was ready for more.

I must have done all right, because Scott had a surprise for me: I'd be doing a second scene later that day with Brittney and a cute redhead with an oddly masculine-sounding name, Felix Vicious, star of *Art School Sluts*, *Goo Girls 9*, and the painful-sounding all-girl flick *Cockless 19*. Strangely, I wasn't exactly looking forward to doing the second scene. Without makeup, Felix, with tattoos and a pierced lip, looked too goth, too young for my tastes. (I'm sure my clean-cut dweebiness didn't do much for her, either.) But glammed up—wow! Too bad I hadn't taken a pill for foot-in-mouth disease: "What a transformation," I told Felix.

She didn't take it as a compliment. "Why?" she said. "Did I look ugly before?"

I'd squandered my chance of building pre-sex rapport with her. Also, my earlier bout with Brittney had worn me out. While napping during lunch, I came up with a brilliant scheme for "sleeping" through the next scene. I told Scott to make it a fantasy sequence in which the two girls "rape" me while I'm dreaming on the couch. "You lazy bastard," Scott said, good-naturedly. "Get off your ass and do those babes like a man."

I put my mask back on.

The scene was more fun than I expected. First, I got to direct Brittney and Felix in a bit of lesbo play. They did my favorite move, the "scissors" position, where girls straddle each other and grind their sweet spots together. I always explode when hot chicks do a scissors on video. But I reminded myself that this was the beginning of a live scene that I had to perform in. It took all my recently gained self-control to wrench my hand from my little sword, and just sit back for a moment and enjoy this display of sapphic delight.

Next, the girls roughed me up a bit. Ms. Vicious lived up to her name, spitting on me and not-so-gently choking me with my own tie, which had been strategically placed on the floor next to the bed. Who knew that asphyxiation and a saliva shower could be such a rush?

Still, it didn't compare to the thrill of drilling Felix. She let out a series of convincing caterwauls as her inner walls pulsed tighter and tighter around me. The only thing that could have added to my excitement would have been switching off between Felix and Brittney. But when I made the request, Brittney, always the pro, said that she'd already done the one intercourse scene that she'd been paid for. It was only a minor disappointment, though, and just meant more time inside Felix. And unlike that morning, I didn't blow my load prematurely. In fact, this time I had the opposite problem. Despite the wonderful sensation of rocking to and fro with Felix's legs wrapped around me, I couldn't come. The girls, both experienced professionals, knew what to do, though. They peeled off my condom and finished me off with some expert handiwork.

My money shot, however, wasn't very photogenic. A few drops of my white stuff just sort of dribbled out. Some of the crew didn't believe I came. But the proof's in the video. All you have to do is magnify the frame one or two hundred times and you can see it.

I returned to New York on Valentine's Day. Unfortunately, my stint as a porn stud couldn't change the fact that on this most romantic of days, I had no girl waiting for me at home. But I figured out how to keep a bit of the glory alive. In the days that followed, I visited a few video stores, wandering the adult sections until I chanced upon a box cover of Brittney or Felix. Then I'd tell the nearest guy, "You're not gonna believe it, but I just slept with her." I was right: they didn't believe it.

I also went back to that bar where I'd met the supposed lesbian in the tight sweater. I showed her a picture of me cavorting with Brittney.

"You're the guy in the mask?" she asked, incredulously.

"That's right."

"You're dreaming." There was no convincing this shrew. She crumpled up the picture and stuffed it in my drink.

It felt good to be home again.

CHAPTER THIRTEEN

Celibate at Sexpo (But Not by Choice)

I wasn't always as lucky with porn stars as I was when I did the Mask. At the end of 2004, I was looking forward to the *Adult Video News* Awards and Adult Entertainment Expo in Las Vegas. I like to call it "Sexpo" for short. It just rolls off the tongue better.

The trade show portion of Sexpo is held each January at the Sands Convention Center at the Venetian. It's an indication of porn's mainstream clout that one of Sin City's swankiest hotels plays host to the adult industry's biggest gathering. Sexpo is ideal for watching porn actresses prancing around the lobby in bustiers and thongs just inches away from families on vacation. The toddlers couldn't care less, but their dads' eyes keep popping out of their heads. The wives, in turn, glare at their husbands, as if they're thinking, "Go ahead, prick. Let's see how horny you feel when I take the house and half your money." It's when I see couples like that I'm glad I've chosen the life I lead. All the sex I want and no one to answer to when I look at a pretty girl.

My holiday season provided a colorful lead-up to Sexpo. On New Year's Eve, I'd gone to the Voyeur's Ball in New York featuring Jenna Jameson. The party was thrown by "Skin," a self-described upscale erotic-lifestyle group (a fancy way of saying swingers club) that organizes events around the country. Such parties were almost exclusively for couples and "adventurous" single girls. Single men were persona non grata. Being a porn journalist certainly had its advantages. I was writing about the party for *Oui*, a hardcore magazine started by Hugh Hefner in the seventies to compete with *Penthouse*. At the time, I was doing a monthly column for *Oui* under the headline "Adventures of an Average Joe." *Oui* may no longer have been part of the *Playboy* publishing empire, but it still had enough cache to score me an invite to the Voyeur's Ball.

Jenna Jameson was just the icing on the cake at a party that had loads of delectable women in their sexy New Year's best. Most of them had dates, but I met a trio of hot bi-babes—a stripper and two stockbrokers—who came to scope other ladies.

"We'd love to hook up with Jenna and do her back at her hotel," the stripper, Rachel, told me.

This could be my best New Year's ever, I thought. Ms. Jameson has always been outspoken about her carpet-munching proclivities. And these were just the kind of party girls that could stir Jenna's juices. I'm in the driver's seat, I thought. I didn't know Jenna, but with my *Oui* credentials, I was sure I could finagle an introduction. Then if Rachel and her friends carried the ball from there, perhaps we'd all get invited back to the then-reigning porn queen's suite.

"I'd be happy to introduce you," I told Rachel.

Donna, one of the stockbrokers, told me she'd love to do porn. "I want to be able to prove when I'm ninety how hot I was when I was young," she said. "But it ain't gonna happen. My father would disown me."

But despite her pornographic reservations, Donna was a real pragmatist. "Maybe you can take private photos of me," she said. "You can show me all glammed up in real sexy outfits in a hot setting, like on a huge bed with satin sheets."

Like many people, she made the natural assumption that as a reporter, I knew something about photography. And she was so enthusiastic that I didn't have the heart to tell her I was a lousy shutterbug.

"It would be an honor," I said. I'm still waiting for her to set the date.

I had a more immediate disappointment when Donna and her gal pals decided to bail before Jenna Jameson arrived at the party. The fantasy would not be fulfilled. But as a consolation prize, I did get to watch them take turns making out with a cute Middle Eastern chick on the dance floor.

I arrived in Vegas the following week with high hopes for a bigger payoff. A British porn journalist friend of mind calls Sexpo "the biggest convention of bimbos where you won't be getting laid." I had hoped in vain to prove him wrong.

As a reporter, I'd already met a shitload of people in the adult industry—producers, directors, publicists, and, of course, performers. Also, I kept telling myself, porn actresses are no different from the prostitutes I'd met in Rio. Cultural differences aside, these were women who liked sex, and who got paid for being promiscuous. If Juliana and Betina could fall for me, then at Sexpo, where there were countless porn stars, I was bound to hook up with at least one or two—maybe at the same time.

The key thing was that I'd be around these girls when they were partying; like Betina the night we'd met. Even off-duty porn stars have needs. It would be so easy, I figured, to get laid in these circumstances.

Ironically, my best chance came not with a performer, but with Julie, a big-breasted Latina who ran an adult video store in Chicago. I was at the Venetian's Circle Bar, the watering hole at the center of the casino floor, when I noticed her gesturing to me from across the bar. I jumped at her invitation.

After a few hours of drinking, we went with her girlfriends up to the suite of a young director/performer. Including his friends, there were eight of us hanging out on his huge bed. Seemed like a perfect porn scene in the making, but Julie wasn't as flirty with me now. Several days of non-stop partying had apparently caught up with her. Also, I'd developed a nasty cold, and my nose wouldn't stop running.

Still, I did my best to keep the momentum going by taking Julie over to the couch. We kissed until she fell asleep with my tongue in her mouth. She woke up and we kissed again, but I had to stop when my nostrils started gushing again like Niagara Falls.

Suddenly, the lights went off, and something more bizarre distracted us. We heard moaning and giggling from the other side of the room. It was just light enough to make out lots of motion on the bed. Julie and I were on the fringes of an orgy. I'd never been in an orgy, mostly due to my one cock rule. Being so close to the action, however, made me want to fuck Julie even more. It's tough, though, when you're devoting all your energy to grabbing tissues one after the other in a losing battle against your nose.

There'd be no second chance with Julie, who went home that morning.

Another girl I met at Sexpo, Angel Fallen (yep—that's the *nom de porn* she picked), was there trying to break into the business.

"Why do you want to get into porn?" I asked.

She said she was fed up with "relationship sex" and wanted to "get better at casual sex." A true gentleman would have offered to help her refine her casual-sex skills right then and there, or at least given her an opportunity to demonstrate what she'd learned thus far. Instead, I merely hung out with her, meekly playing slots. We were right near the bathrooms, too, which the Venetian always kept in pristine condition. How easy it would have been to romp with Angel in one of the stalls. Sure, there are always the "eye in the sky" security cameras, but their priority is identifying scammers at the tables, not horny guests grinding against each other in the john. And on the off chance that a bored security guard might come knocking on the stall door, it would have been worth the risk. But I never shared my idea with Angel, so I'll never know what "could have, would have, should have" happened with her.

More opportunities for scoring at Sexpo came via my friendship with porn actor Dino Bravo. During the convention, he was hired to do a video with Lexxy Foxx, a statuesque blonde MILF with a fondness for mai tais. She asked me if I was going to be in the scene. When I told her that I was just there to write about it for *Oui*, she said, "Too bad. You should be in it."

It took me a moment to figure out the implications of what she was saying. If I was in the scene, I'd get to bang her. My neural circuits went into a frenzy trying to calculate the best strategy for convincing the director to put me in it. I had a great pitch, too, as I reasoned it would translate to more publicity for him and the film. Where were my balls when I needed them? In the end, I didn't say a word. I simply basked in the glory of Lexxy's comment.

I did take part in one porn scene, however. It was for Scottish filmmaker "Gazzman" (even those behind the camera use stage names in porn), the prior year's *Adult Video News* award winner for best foreign director. He paired me up with luscious uber-titted blonde Brooke Haven, who gave me on-camera instruction on how to get her off with a pocket rocket. I also got to stick my digits in Ms. Haven's honey pot, but that was it. "You have no idea how fuckin' jealous my cock is of my fingers," I told her.

CHAPTER FOURTEEN

Oxygen

A FEW SUMMERS AGO, CUSTOMS AGENTS AT PALM BEACH INTERnational Airport netted a curious big fish, Rush Limbaugh, returning from the Dominican Republic with Viagra prescribed to someone else. For mongers, it was the same as spotting the conservative radio host in a brothel with his wallet out and his pants down. Sex-tourism websites went into overdrive as mongers shared their "certainty" that Limbaugh had been partaking in the island nation's pay-for-play sex scene.

Sex tourism is huge in the Dominican Republic. In certain cities, even car washes serve as fronts for brothels.

In recent years, the Dominican Republic has seen the rise of all-inclusive, full-service resorts. Club Meds, if you will, for mongers. They include high-end luxury spots like Viking's Exotic Resort and Oxygen Retreat. With their focus on discretion and selection of attractive, educated young women who specialize in delivering the GFE, such resorts might well represent mongering's future, at least for gringos with deep pockets.

My first visit to the Dominican Republic was on assignment for *Club* magazine to report on the making of a porn film. It was the first time I met Gazzman, the flick's director. We became friends and I subsequently ended up doing some public relations work for his side venture, Porn Week, which provides porn fans front-row seats at adult film sets in exotic locations around the world. Porn Week attendees were here now to see Gazzman shoot at Viking's, where guests paid upwards of $1,000 daily for a new female companion every day. Most of the escorts were from Eastern Europe, as were some of Gazzman's actresses, who I should point out were here strictly to shoot porn, and had nothing to do with Viking's.

The girls at Oxygen, on the other hand, were all mine for the taking. *Hustler* sent me there on my favorite kind of assignment: not to cover a porn shoot, but to serve as a "reconnaissance man" for our readers by availing myself of all the amenities the resort had to offer. How else would they know whether Oxygen was worth their readers' time or money? These are the kind of fact-finding missions at which I truly excel.

My piece on Oxygen went on to win me the coveted "Smutty" award from the Smut Journalists of America, so, if you'll indulge me, I think the opening paragraph, bears repeating:

"You're sipping a martini at a tiki bar surrounded by palm trees, a blazing orange sun setting in the distance. A pair of stunning Latinas with nothing but towels around their waists are entertaining you. Their caramel-colored skin glistens and their nipples rub against you as they nibble on your ear and molest you through your bathing suit. You fucked one of these dark-haired temptresses last night, though all that free booze makes it hard to remember which one.

No problem. You can refresh your memory an hour from now, when you're fucking both of them."

The resort, a short flight from Miami, is on the Dominican Republic's north coast. It's got a great tropical climate free of the hurricanes that batter other parts of the island.

I arrived at this real-life Fantasy Island half-expecting a pudgy-faced midget ("de plane, boss, de plane") and a mysterious gentleman in an elegant white suit to welcome me. Instead, I was greeted by Oxygen's smoking-hot hostesses. These girls do a lot more than put a mint on your pillow. "Our girls understand the meaning of 'full service,'" said Mike, one of the resort's owners.

Mike and his colleague Robert opened Oxygen in September 2006. The former strip-club operators had learned plenty about catering to men's fantasies. "We're regular guys who've done the single and married thing and decided to create an exclusive resort where men's fantasies can come true, where you can enjoy the companionship of women selected not only for their looks, but also their personality and cleanliness," said Mike.

"We'd checked out the escort scene around the world," he added. "Regardless of location—Southeast Asia, Eastern Europe, Latin America—at least 80 percent of the women were not that attractive or just hustlers with no real interest in providing a good time. Also, in a lot of these countries we couldn't find good food or it was extremely expensive."

I'd certainly take issue with the Latin America part, especially if he's including Brazilian women. And food in Rio is incredibly cheap, if you don't mind filling up on skewered beef from pushcarts or greasy, but delicious, ham and cheese *joelhos* at the city's many sandwich counters. But I couldn't argue with the quality of the girls he'd recruited for Oxygen. Nor the cuisine. The lobster and filet mignon proved that.

I also couldn't complain about the quantity of women. There were about forty girls at the resort that weekend—plenty of entertainment for its twenty guests. The girls included local babes, Asians, South Americans, and Eastern Europeans. And instead of the bottom-feeders Mike had encountered in his travels, Oxygen had cherry-picked the best of the bunch.

Many of the girls who come to work at the resort are college students. They can pull in anywhere from $1,500 to $3,500 in a week working at Oxygen.

Your cash is no good here. Instead, you get a booklet filled with tickets when you check in. A blue ticket is worth a two-hour session with a girl of your choice, and a green ticket an all-nighter (*toda la noche*, in sexed-up Spanish).

All monies are, of course, paid beforehand. Prices start at $1,995 for a three day, two night stay. That gets you all the food and drink you can handle, and enough tickets to bump uglies with up to four girls a day. Is it worth it? That would depend on your values. As I wrote for *Hustler*: "One guy might prefer to put his money toward a big plasma TV so he can sit at home and jack off to lifelike images. Another chooses to spend it on the real thing at an erotic El Dorado like Oxygen where the pussy's worth its weight in gold."

Oxygen seems to be pulling enough repeat business to justify its business plan. "I found Oxygen through a search engine using 'sex vacation' or 'adult vacation,'" recalls loyal customer Brian, sixty-one, who's been there five times since March 2007. "Once you've been there and return the girls are very friendly with you and greet you at the door with a big hug and kisses."

Brian's first girl at Oxygen was La Bebe (which means "the baby"), a buxom eighteen-year-old Dominicana. "The last time I had sex with an eighteen-year-old I think I was nineteen," says Brian. "I am a breast man so that tends to factor in my selection and the friendlier the better."

His last trip, Brian enjoyed a foursome "happy hour" that might have cemented his loyalty to Oxygen for years to come.

"I was having a drink at the bar," he says. "A number of girls, five or six, were sitting in the ping pong area and one called out 'Brian, happy hour.' So I went over and asked in my best Spanish, '*Todos?*' They laughed and Jenifer said 'lesbian show' so I thought to myself, what will I be doing while that's going on? I decided to take three of them back to my room which started with [all] of us in the shower then went to the bed. Jenifer proceeded to eat out another girl while the third one gave me a blow job. I came about the same time as the girl so we changed positions and I ate the girl that gave me the blow job while the other two switched positions."

"The foursome has been on my mind since I got back." Brian plans to return for the July 4 weekend and work "on variations and possibly a fivesome."

Paul, a financial advisor in his mid-fifties from Maryland told me he "pretty much had sex the entire time" he was there. His favorite was a girl named Argentina. "She kind of became my girlfriend for the last day. I am going back in June to see her, hopefully she will still be there. . . . It was difficult to choose who to go with because I wanted a lot of the ladies. I liked Argentina because she was a little shy, as am I." Paul got the chance to break out of his shell at Oxygen. "I had five or six other girls during my stay and had a three-on-one . . . which was without a doubt the craziest thing I have ever done. I felt like [the girls] didn't even need me there, I mean they were really into each other doing things I have only read about in *Penthouse Forum*."

"I learned about Oxygen from a couple of other guys I met at Viking's," says Anthony, a husky electrician from New York. Besides the amount of girls, he was impressed with "the hassle-free feeling of never having to tip. I had like five orgies in four days; it was the wildest time of my life. . . . My memories are forever embedded in my brain, at least until next time I go."

Anthony says that at Viking's, "there was a huge language barrier because Russian sounds nothing like English. At least Spanish was close. At Oxygen I was pretty much getting raped on a daily basis. . . . I thought Viking's was pretty fun until I went to Oxygen. . . . The Latin women are more into the sex, especially with each other where at Viking's it felt like a professional Vegas-type experience. The shows at night at Oxygen were almost too much for me to watch, and I mean that in the best way. I have never seen a lesbian show like that, I almost fell off my chair." Anthony had some lively encounters in the pool, noting that "the ladies get frisky in them. . . . But most importantly the ladies are around you all the time and treat you like you would want to be treated. . . . [Oxygen] was not only great but truly the time of my life and I will always be a customer even if I decide to get married again."

After the *Hustler* article came out, I got tons of emails from people who wanted to know more. TL, who'd just booked a trip to Oxygen, asked, "Do you get to cum as many times as you want" during a session? "Great question," I responded. "The girls have to stay with you the whole session. As far as how many times you actually fuck during a session, that might be something you decide with each girl individually." I advised him to ask the girl before he takes her back to the room if she's cool with fucking an indeterminate number of times. "If she seems hesitant, NEXT!! Plenty of women there to choose from."

He also wanted to know if Oxygen girls "really get into the threesomes, and would it be possible to have a foursome?"

"The girls I had a threesome with were into it big-time," I wrote him. "But I definitely suggest speaking to all the girls at Oxygen beforehand (as well as other guys there) to get a feel for who's truly into other girls as opposed to being 'gay for pay.' You can have as many girls as you want simultaneously, as long as you have enough coupons."

TL had shelled out a nice chunk of change for the villa and wanted to know if he'd get his money's worth. "It's definitely worth the money if you 'put into it' as much as you want to get out of it," I replied. "By that I mean take time to talk to the girls a bit beforehand so you can get a sense of how playful/sexy/fun they'll be when you're fucking their brains out. I'm sure you know this already, but the hottest-looking girl (at Oxygen or any place, for that matter) isn't always the greatest in bed. Of course many times the hottest girl *is* amazing in bed, but ultimately, it's luck of the draw; I don't know which girls will be at Oxygen when you're there, so it's hard to generalize."

The advice applies to any sex haven. If sex in and of itself won't satisfy you, you have to window shop. I formed a guideline in Rio that the hotter the girl was—which usually meant a higher asking price—the more she had to prove she was worth it. Call it Joe's Law of Inverse Hotness. I really think that if a girl's too attractive, she comes to think that just her mere presence is enough. But I can't fuck a sculpture or a photo in a dirty magazine. I need flesh and blood. A 10 on the hotness scale automatically drops to a 6 or 7 if she's cold. Conversely, a 6 or 7 leaps to a 9 or 10 if she has charisma, animation, and passion.

Says Brian: "I find that at times the girls pick you rather than the other way around and I'm not one to say no to a pretty girl."

"The girls actually 'rape' you there," adds Anthony. "They really like having sex. If it's an act then they should all get Academy Awards, because they were so into each other. I could just sit back and watch, which was a huge turn-on as well. I thought all of the girls were gorgeous so I let them choose me."

All the Oxygen guests when I was there were men, though the resort allows couples, too, and is definitely swinger-friendly. Most of the guys I spoke to were single, like Zak, a computer programmer from New York. Some were married, away on "business."

"You got everything you need pretty much at Oxygen," Zak says. "You got the pool, you got the restaurant, the bar. . . . I don't go to the gym, but it's there."

And of course there's the number one attraction: "The girls are beautiful, nice, friendly," says Zak.

Guys young enough to fight in Iraq were partying at Oxygen alongside men who were old enough to have killed Nazis. Thank

God the girls didn't span the generations. Their average age was around twenty.

Like Elena, a luscious little spinner from Venezuela. The morning after our night together, someone knocked on my door at 7 a.m. My aggravation quickly changed to excitement when it turned out to be Mika, a beautiful Filipina with platinum hair down to her ass (nothing says "fuck me" like an Asian Barbie), and a lip-smacking tattoo of Angelina Jolie on her shoulder. Mika was here to gather Elena for their English course downtown.

"Wanna join us for a few minutes?" I asked.

"If it's okay with Elena."

Before I had a chance to ask, Elena was at my side. She took Mika's hand. "I don't mind at all," she said.

The two Oxygen babes went to town on each other, "ignoring" me just the way I liked in these situations. When they finally pulled me into the act, it was too late: Mika just had to touch me and I erupted.

Another time, Mika and I were in the pool with top-heavy (and topless) Latina goddess La Bebe. She was sloshing up a storm. "I'm still learning to swim," she said. She really didn't need to. Her artificial flotation devices would have made the Titanic unsinkable.

Over by the waterfall, Mika pulled me under the pool's surface and kissed me. On the way up, we smacked into La Bebe's boobs. "I'm shielding your heads from the waterfall," she said.

It was all the foreplay I could handle. I asked the girls to meet back at my room. La Bebe couldn't make it, but Mika showed up in a white lace bustier, garters and G-string. She treated me to a mouthwatering striptease.

As we got into my Jacuzzi, she asked why my bathing suit was still on. The girl had no respect for my inherent modesty, taking it upon herself to remove the garment with her nimble toes. Her fancy footwork inspired me to rub her sweet spot with my big toe. That, coupled with the Jacuzzi's powerful jet, had Mika moaning in no time.

With Mika on the loose, Oxygen didn't need any other hurricanes. Her inhaling and exhaling on my dick generated enough gale-force winds to rip the island in two.

Zak was also blown away by how insatiable the girls were. Even the ones with boyfriends seemed like nymphomaniacs, he noted. "It's not like they're not getting enough over there, but they're still running around with their fucking vibrators and playing with each other and themselves when clients aren't available."

After a few trips, Zak surmised: "I'd say 99 percent of the girls at Oxygen that I went with were totally into it and couldn't wait to get whatever kind of action they could. They love a lot of penetration but they also love a little 'tongue lashing' and all that sort of stuff."

But as overwhelmingly enthusiastic as the vast majority of the women at Oxygen were, Zak and I both encountered Lena, a girl who was a "little bit hesitant" in bed. We compared notes.

"You can sense it, you can feel it," Zak said. "I mean, she still went through with it. But you know she didn't really want to."

"Lena can't fuck to save her life," he continued. "She's a sweet girl and all. Don't get me wrong. But she is fucking killing me. When I'm down there, she's cockblocking me left and right. She likes to hang onto me."

But in the room, she always complains that Zak's hurting her. She thinks that jiggling a bit in bed is all that's required to satisfy her partner. "I'm like, what the fuck? Are we fucking here or what? Or are we just dancing?"

Zak recalls a threesome he had with Lena and another girl, Daria. As he was fucking Lena, the other girl was "lying on her back next to us, fingering herself," horny as hell.

"All of a sudden Lena starts cracking up, laughing her head off," says Zak. "I'm like, what the fuck?" Lena had destroyed the mood. "She fucking killed it."

I had a similar buzz-killer with Lena and another girl. Lena seemed so damn uncomfortable just being touched by the other girl, that I felt myself overcome with pity for her. After a few minutes, I stopped the ménage, telling Lena that it was okay. She could just hang out and chill. I did continue fucking the other girl, though, and Lena thankfully kept to herself.

On another occasion, Zak took her to his room, but told her, "Listen. We're just going to go to bed, we're going to watch some TV, then go to sleep. And that's that."

After his trip to Oxygen, TL emailed me to say: "I just wanted to thank you for one of the greatest times in my life. I walked in and was greeted by a very generous staff. I saw some of the most gorgeous women in the world . . . yum yum . . . had some of the best food I have ever had in my life, and I live in San Francisco, a food capital. I had the paella, and the lamb chops. Shoot, I would go back just for the food."

What did TL think of the girls?

"Sitting there the ladies started speaking Spanish as if I did not understand," he says. "I understand a lot but speak a little. They were saying that I was young and great looking, which made me blush. I started to ask them their names in Spanish and they were shocked to learn that this white guy could speak good Spanish. I was still unsure what I could and could not do. Then one lady walked up to me (about five foot seven, all legs and gorgeous like Halle Berry), grabbed my ass and asked me if I wanted to see her later that I night. I was shocked to have this perfect 10 walk right up to me and basically molest me in the dining room. I had the time of my life and I am already planning to go back in March. To see how the girls moved their hips when the music was on at the bar, I was drooling the entire time I was there. And they loved me for the fact that I spoke Spanish to them."

TL also mentioned meeting a guest from Chicago who said he'd been "scared to come down, but your article convinced him to come, and now he will be back at least once a year." I love it when my words inspire others, even if I'm inspiring them toward a life of mongering.

CHAPTER FIFTEEN

Thai High

AT THE LEGENDARY EDEN CLUB IN BANGKOK, A YELLOW LINE running from the ceiling to the floor divides the bar into two camps: girls who'll do anal, and girls who won't. If you go for the former, you might want to clean off with a "soapy massage." Sex-travel websites call this relaxing pastime "one of Thailand's greatest treasures," where beautiful women "bathe you, and then lather you up on an air mattress for a full body massage. After you are thoroughly cleaned you move to the bed for some incredible hot sex."

When it comes to Thai sexcapades, my fellow monger, Zak, is the King of Siam. (I hope to follow in his footsteps when the royalties from this book start pouring in.) I met him at Oxygen, where he eagerly posed for photos with the Oxygen girls for the article I wrote for *Hustler*.

Zak came to the U.S. from southwest Germany, near Stuttgart, at seventeen. He went to college here, returned home, and moved here permanently in 1991. He's never married.

"I had a few girlfriends," he said. "But nothing like—well, the first one was the one that broke my heart and then after that you kind of numb off a little bit I guess." His relationships in America have typically lasted "a few months."

Zak hasn't dated many Americans. He doesn't like going through the "dating shit," the wining and dining, before getting laid. "I've got my issues with American girls," he said. He's not sure if overseas prostitutes have jaded him, or if it's "just impatience."

He was in his mid-twenties the first time he had sex with a prostitute, at a brothel in his hometown. "Over there it's nothing. It's very common over there because it's legal so you don't even think about it. You've got brothels all over the place and you can pick girls up off the street as well. So it's really not a big deal over there." The German public, he said, is much more accepting of prostitution than Americans. "Of course not for married people. That's a different story."

Such tolerance doesn't guarantee great sex, however. The five-story brothel was "a little bit cold," he recalled. "You walked through a corridor, girls were sitting in open-door rooms watching TV waiting for clients. You go in, girls are like, what do you want? They were very businesslike. Nothing like the Dominican Republic," he said. He's had hookers in South Africa, Vegas, Los Angeles, and New York, but his best experiences have been in the Dominican Republic and Brazil. Zak now goes to Germany about once a year, and visited a brothel near his town on one of his recent visits. The place was strictly for locals, not tourists. He paid fifty euros for fifteen minutes. "The last one I actually couldn't wait to get out of there, because she was cold. She actually complained about the smell of cum so I said 'get the fuck out of here.' She says 'thank God for the Febreze.' She keeps spraying it . . . . I'm like 'Oh Jesus, let me get out of here.'"

His experiences in Thailand, which he visited five times between 2003 and 2005, were more compelling, His first trip was a birthday gift from his brother. "I really didn't know what to expect over there because I'd never been to Asia before," he said. "And I kind of liked it."

But just how did Thailand become known as the "brothel of the world"? The story begins with a consideration of the Thai government's blundered efforts against child prostitution and pedophile sex tourists. Despite recent successes, it is no question that the country still has an image problem. Note, for example, the unfounded horror stories that traffickers were preying on children in the wake of the tsunami that devastated Southeast Asia in late 2004. The international media was particularly drawn to a rumor— later proven untrue—that a twelve-year-old Swedish boy who'd been in Thailand with his family during the catastrophe was snatched from a hospital.

The tsunami might not have caused an upsurge in trafficking, but it landed a heavy blow on Patong Beach, a mongering playground on Thailand's Phuket island. The damage reportedly diverted flocks of mongers to Bangkok. Ironically, a drought and a poor rice crop in northeastern Thailand around this time caused more girls than usual to seek sex work in the Thai capital. Earlier generations of young women from poor villages had poured into Bangkok during the Vietnam War for similar reasons. That's when American GIs on leave helped to establish Thailand as the "brothel of the world," not that the soldiers were defiling a pristine culture. Thailand has a long history of prostitution. Reportedly, more than half of all Thai men lose their virginity to prostitutes, and more than 400,000 visit brothels each day. But like many statistics relating to the sex trade, we have to take these with a grain of salt.

Paying for sex has technically been illegal in Thailand since 1960, but the Entertainment Places Act of 1966 helped the government tap into the visiting GIs' rest and recreation dollars by allowing massage parlors, go-go bars, and the like to essentially serve as brothels. Chuwit Kamolvisit, a former member of parliament and one of the country's most controversial figures, owns a chain of Bangkok massage parlors that he bluntly calls "semen collection centers." Even a military coup in 2006 failed to have an appreciable impact on Thailand's sex trade.

A law proposed in 2003 would openly legalize prostitution. The idea is still being debated.

For Zak, it didn't start out as a mongering trip, though. He went with his brother, his brother's girlfriend, and a few male friends.

They were in Hua Hin, a tourist town a few hours south of Bangkok on the west coast of the Gulf of Thailand when he met Nit, a working girl.

"It's got a small little center, just one bar after the other," Zak said. "And of course, you know each bar has their girls, their regular girls that come over there and hang out. And then you just hang out in the bar, have your beers, they're coming up to you, you buy them a drink. And normally the way it goes, if you want to take them with you to the hotel, you've got to pay the bar what they call a bar fine. Of course we were too cheap. We said 'Nah, I don't want to.' So we walked away and I told Nit I'd meet her outside."

She was thirty, "a lot older than I actually thought. I could have sworn she wasn't any older than twenty-four. But that's the way they are down there, they keep themselves in good shape. Nit had a son who lived with her parents on a farm."

Hardly fluent in English, Nit could communicate what Zak called "everyday stuff" like let's eat, let's go here, etc.

Why did he go with Nit? Besides her white teeth, her beautiful black hair, and the fact that she smiled that sweet smile at him?

"She was the first one I met down there and she never left me alone," he said. "So I never really had to go anywhere else." She definitely had a hold on him. "I went down there again to see her. Then she became very possessive . . . at the same time she wants everything but she pushes you away a little bit."

What made you want to keep going back? I asked.

"She was very sweet. In the beginning. It was almost like a girlfriend."

The classic GFE. She was even affectionate in public, holding his hand, kissing him spontaneously. But over time, she grew colder.

Sex with Nit "was okay. She was very good, she was very nice. The only thing is, well, she always said 'I'm a little shy.' That kind of pissed me off a little bit. But she always wanted to fuck, there was no question about it."

She didn't like to fuck with the lights on, though, because of her shyness. She also didn't like giving head. "So it was always a battle." When she gave head, she wasn't very good. "She was just good really at just fucking."

Zak's had other Thai girls that "were really into it. But they didn't hang onto me like that." After the night was done, "they disappeared."

"I'm comfortable with what I know, so I kind of like it when they're like a girlfriend," he said. But at the same time, he enjoys girls who are wild, not mild, in bed.

That first trip, Zak and Nit spent a few days together. When he told her he was leaving for Koh Samui, another tourist spot and Thailand's third-largest island, she became a drama queen. "Of course," Zak said, "now she puts the fucking tears up and all this sort of stuff." He was on the beach in Koh Samui when she texted him, asking him where he was staying. "Two hours later she knocked on my door. That's why I'm saying, they don't leave you alone."

At the start, she might have had genuine feelings for him. But ultimately, Zak's convinced, it was all about the money.

"She kept calling me, even after I left. She calls me, she's crying. But that's all a show."

He hooked up with her again when he returned to Thailand later that year. Nit told him that her mother was very sick. Soon, she said she needed money for her mom.

Zak gave Nit money a number of times. But when she kept asking, he became exasperated. Zak said she'd come to him with a variety of "sob stories," including once when she claimed that somebody had stolen her backpack at the beach.

"As soon as you move on, she's like, 'Oh, send me money, send me money.'"

On his next visit, a business trip, Nit clung to him like a vine. "Of course, she picks you up from the airport and she drops you off at the airport. Because they want to make sure that you're not seeing anyone else."

In that way, Nit reminds me of Juliana, my Rio lunachick. One time in Koh Samui, Zak tried to shake Nit loose. He pulled the old monger stunt of claiming that he had to fly home a day earlier before his actual return, so he needed to go back to Bangkok. When she said she'd go back to the capital with him, he responded that he didn't have money to fly her there. She got emotional, but accepted it.

Zak thought he'd gained himself a free day in Bangkok to monger with his friends. He picked up a nineteen-year-old at Soi Cowboy, a popular go-go bar. "She let me know she wasn't looking for a relationship," Zak said. She agreed to stay for the night, but had to leave at 6 a.m. for college. She was down to earth, and didn't make a production about wanting to stay in touch with him. Like me, he liked girls, even pros (especially pros) who had something else going for them—like college, or a more-mainstream job. For me, it's one of the ultimate fantasies. A hooker on her way to better things. A "dirty" sex freak who'll be off the market soon, available to no one but you. Nit had told him, "Give me money, I'll go to school." He'd given her some money for that purpose, but she hadn't gone to school.

At 9 a.m., the Do Not Disturb sign notwithstanding, there was a knock on Zak's door. He yelled at the unknown culprit to get lost. A few minutes later, the front desk called to say someone was there to see him, that he should open the door. Despite his protests that he was sleeping and didn't want any visitors, the knocking resumed. Finally, he dragged his ass out of bed to see Nit through the peephole. As I had with Juliana, he raced through the room cleaning up all signs of the other girl—cigarette butts, hairs, etc. When he let her in, she immediately launched into a top-to-bottom inspection of the room that included the closets, under the bed, and the bathroom.

She didn't find any evidence. Instead, she busted him on lying about his return date. "I don't know what I said," he told me. "I wanted to spend time with friends. What's the big deal?"

For the record, Zak said that he really did like Nit, but he couldn't deal with all the histrionics. Here she was, so jealous. Yet she had no problem fucking other guys when Zak was overseas. "I understand that," he told me. But she wanted it all, and it wasn't going to work that way.

Zak could get jealous, too. One night, he was shooting pool with Nit and her girlfriends. At 1 a.m., he was tired and wanted to go back to the room. She said she was staying.

He thinks she'd started taking drugs. That's what one of her girlfriends told him, though he admits the friend, also a prostitute, might have had an ulterior motive, like trying to steal him away.

Once, however, before they left on a trip to Singapore, she acted odd, refusing to let Zak come in her bedroom as she got some things.

On that visit to Thailand, he hadn't told her he was coming. Instead, he decided to surprise her by showing up at the hair salon where she was supposed to be working for extra cash. She wasn't there. He called her. When she arrived, "she was pretty cold." The surprise had backfired. Still, they spent a few weeks together, including the trip to Singapore. It was her first time out of Thailand. After a few days, she was homesick, particularly for Thai food.

The reality is that I'm just as prone to GFEs as Zak seems to be. Doesn't take much to make me thank God that I've met someone "special" who I want to spend tons of time with—but perhaps it was a good thing he ultimately wasn't able to get her a U.S. tourist visa. The strict requirements had discouraged him. Instead he tried for a German visa. That should have been a slam dunk, but her application was rejected. He asked a girl at the German embassy why. Apparently, Nit had said all the wrong things, like that her son didn't live with her, which made her seem more of a risk. Zak thinks that she blew her chances on purpose, that she really didn't want to go with him to Europe.

A number of her girlfriends had gone to the States or Europe to be with foreign guys, usually only for a few months. Why did they return? Either their patron didn't care to extend their visa, or the culture shock of cold weather, food, etc., was too much for them.

Nit wanted stability, "but on her own terms," said Zak. That meant staying in Thailand, not living abroad with a foreigner.

Zak went with Nit to her hometown, an eight-hour bus ride from Bangkok. Though he was introduced as Nit's boyfriend, Zak thinks her parents knew what she did. In some of these poorer countries, he says families might even expect their daughters to hook in order to bring in money.

At its best, Zak's adventures with Nit and her family seemed more like those of a cultural exchange student than a pure sex tour.

Zak doesn't see himself getting married. For now, he's having too much fun mongering abroad. But he wouldn't have a problem marrying a prostitute, as long as she stopped hooking.

Have prostitutes spoiled him on having a conventional relationship? Probably, he says. "The thing is, I've seen too many relationships go bad. And it hurts a lot. Not only my own, but also friends and family. What's the point? I'm having a good time. I'm not missing anything. I'm happy. I'm busy all day anyway while I'm working. And I don't need somebody to call me every half hour and say, 'When are you coming home?' I'm married to my business."

Still, he doesn't rule out settling down someday. About regular girls, he says: "If I get the commitment, I would give it. I would be willing to give it, but at the same time it's a two-way street . . . I think it's fairly simple. We all have needs, right? If she gives me everything, then I have no need to go out to the Dominican Republic or anywhere else."

Like me, Zak hasn't been shy about telling his platonic female friends about his mongering. "They kind of laugh it off a little bit," he says. One girl he's close with "makes fun of it," kids him about it.

Zak also says he'd tell a girlfriend at home about his escapades abroad. "We all have a history," he said. "I would want to know what she's been doing, you know, what she was up to. Not that I need to know details or anything like that but I would expect a person to be open and I would be open as well. It's a give and take. I would definitely not hide it. Because you know what? You try to hide something, eventually it's going to come out. She's going to find my *Hustler*"—Zak, after all, is one of the stars of my article on Oxygen—"under the mattress."

CHAPTER SIXTEEN

Jeremy's Journeys

JEREMY, A MIDDLE-AGED MUSIC-INDUSTRY EXECUTIVE FROM California, first visited Thailand in the late 1990s. "I'd always been attracted to Asian girls and thought, well, let's go to the headwaters—Thailand," said Jeremy.

In the months leading up to the trip, he'd been corresponding with Asian women who advertised in magazines seeking to meet Americans. These were regular girls looking for relationships, not prostitutes looking for paying clients, Jeremy stressed. He arranged to meet Kanthima, a tall single mother with a red-streaked brown bob in her early twenties from Bangkok.

"It was the idea of going to a tropical environment with a pretty Asian girl that appealed to me," he said.

But while in Bangkok, Jeremy "had the driver from the hotel drive me around to all these different brothels. You walked in [to one place] and there are twenty girls behind a window with a number on them," he recalled.

He wasn't floored, though. "The brothel was very sterile, formulaic, and I didn't like it." Overall, he "hated Bangkok. I couldn't wait to get out of there. It wasn't until subsequent trips that I really kind of got 'it,'" he said, referring to the city and its sex scene.

The skin trade "is part of the fabric of society out there, so you just kind of accept it for what it is," he said.

"But there's also a dark, dark side to this story," he added, recalling a time when he saw a heavyset light-haired man, around fifty, on a boat. "He had a girl with him that looked like she was twelve fucking years old. It just creeped me out."

On Jeremy's first trip, he took the girl and her friend, who served as interpreter, to Koh Samui.

He put the girls up in their own bungalow. "We just hunkered down there for a week," he said. "It was the Thailand fantasy. There are no buildings around, there's nothing but coconut trees and little Thai shacks. And these two girls. There wasn't anybody else at the resort so we basically had the whole place to ourselves. We'd go canoeing, and I got to know this girl."

The intimacy, however, didn't extend beyond making out and snuggling.

"I remember lying there one afternoon, and the girl snuggled up in my arms," said Jeremy. "I'm in my little grass shack with a little cloth over the door, looking out over the South China Sea. And I'm thinking to myself, 'Man, if my friends could see me now.' That is exactly what I thought."

Neither of them wanted to live outside their homelands, though, so the GFE didn't last.

On Jeremy's next trip to Thailand, he went with a friend to Patong, the beach resort that serves as the main tourist spot on Thailand's largest island, Phuket.

"Patong is a fun little beach town," said Jeremy. "It's like Fort Lauderdale, only smaller."

They hit Bangla Road, the heart of Patong's nightlife scene.

"There are bars that are like stalls," he said. "And they're just packed with tourists and working girls, street girls." Among Jeremy's stops was Rock Hard, one of the area's main flesh markets. "The club was primarily for Westerners and was full of bar girls. Really, really cute bar girls. So you'd find one that you liked and you'd pay the house a service fee. Either it was for a long time—which meant that she'd go back to the hotel with you—or a short time—which meant that you'd go to one of the nearby hourly rate hotels, do your business and come back."

Jeremy also checked out Patong's most famous massage parlor (with happy endings, of course), Christin Massage. Located in a big pink building south of Bangla Road, Christin's "is truly a wonderful place," he says. "It's like a little mini-hotel. But each room is wonderfully appointed. They have these great whirlpool baths and really cozy bedrooms. You'd go in there and have a cocktail and pick your girl and pay your fee. And off you'd go."

How would he decide on a girl in Patong? Jeremy told me he likes to keep it simple, not overthink it: Is she cute? Does she seem nice? Then great. One night, he said, "a bar girl, certainly not the cutest one, a little overweight, just glommed onto me."

She told him, "Oh, I just need to make some money. I have to go home to my family in a few days."

"It was a mercy fuck on my part," Jeremy said.

At Patong's upscale clubs, he recalled paying about $100 or less to spend a few days with a girl. "These were like rent-a-girlfriends," he said. "These girls were really cute and really friendly and they pretended they were your girlfriend. All the girls that I hooked up with down there were great. They were fun, they were sweet. And then you were gone. They had fun because we were fun and we did fun things with them and they made good money. And we were decent looking guys. You know, we weren't redneck jerks. I mean you go down to Bangkok, you see the weirdest shit. You see fifty-year-old men holding hands with twenty-year-old girls walking down the street."

"In the mornings we'd send them on their way," Jeremy added. He and his friend would walk the girls through the hotel lobby. "Which was a strange sight, because everybody in the hotel was thinking, 'Look at these fucking guys.'"

He and his friend would hang out by the pool during the day. "Thai girls hate the sun," he said. "There's none of this laying around the pool stuff." They'd meet up with their "rent-a-girlfriends" around 4 p.m.

"For me it wasn't about going down there and having sex," said Jeremy. "It's an adventure. That's how I looked at it. It wasn't just the girls. The girls were a component of it. It's about going to this incredible place that's got fantastic food, palm trees everywhere, a good friend you're traveling with, a beautiful swimming pool to hang out by, a good book to read, and an adventure. And, oh by the way, you can rent a girlfriend while you're there. I have no desire to go and 'sport fuck,'" he added.

Still, Jeremy has stayed clear-eyed about his experiences with Thai pros. He said you really can't compare relationships with everyday American women to prostitutes in Thailand. The latter, he noted, "are being paid to be nice to you. It's not reality. You can't really compare it. Thai women can be very severe. I have no doubt that just like any place else, once the honeymoon is over, things change."

Ah, but while the honeymoon lasts?

"I tell people that everything they've heard about Thailand is true," said Jeremy. "And there are places that are way nastier than where I went to. Pattaya is supposed to be like Sodom and Gomorrah, for God's sake."

Frommer's *Thailand 2007* describes Pattaya as, "all flashing neon and blaring music down to the smallest soi, or side-street, an assault on the senses. Places like the South Pattaya pedestrian area, 'Walking Street,' are lined with open-air watering holes with bar girls luring each passerby: The nightlife finds you in this town with an imploring, 'You, mister, where you go?' Go-go bars are everywhere and red-light 'Bar Beer' joints are springing up as fast as local officials can close them down."

Pattaya also has "Boyz Town," a row of gay go-go clubs and what Frommer's calls "a very active Katoey (transvestite) scene."

All is not fun and games in Pattaya, though. According to Frommer's, "The same debauch that brings so many to Pattaya is pretty sad in the light of day though, when bleary-eyed revelers stumble around streets once glowing with neon, now bleak and strewn with garbage."

I wanted to know if Pattaya lived up to Jeremy's description, so I scanned the monger websites.

"DRRonin" reports on ISG:

"The go-go bars in Bangkok are so dull I practically nod off when I take my rare trips into one. The girls look even more bored than I do most of the time as they dance back and forth from one foot to the other like programmed robots on Quaaludes. The ones in Pattaya usually seem to have a little more energy going for them but mainly of course they have naked nipples and that really makes all the difference. Some of the go-go bars in Bangkok have them I know but the few I have seen in Soi Cowboy are frightful sights and I would gladly pay for them to cover up. The breasts in Pattaya are on average a much finer sampling of young womanhood though it differs dramatically from bar to bar."

At go-go bar Club Boesche, he and his friend "J" enjoyed the live entertainment: "We sat at a small table near the sauna and watched a three-girl nude licking act." "J" was "totally into it, especially when one of them put her head on his lap while being serviced. The waitress next to him was giving a running account of his growing erection."

"Lostlost," a member of of the website Pattaya Secrets, gives a similar account under the topic, "The In-Club Raunch Factor," noting that in some clubs you can expect to find guys eating pussy, close up lesbian shows, along with bar girls inserting ice cubes in their pussies and then trying to shoot the ice into your drink. He said his friend had a bar girl pull down his pants and suck his cock for about twenty seconds at one of these places. Give a girl 100 baht [about $3] and anything goes.

Another contributor to Pattaya Secrets says the raunchiest bar he went to was the Windmill. The power went off and two girls jumped right into his lap. He said it felt like a Punch and Judy show as both girls were bouncing up and down on both of his hands. He was double-holing, and double-digiting each of their holes.

Aside from the shows, DRRonin doesn't sound too impressed with Pattaya. "It sounds absurd but there are just too many women here," he posts. "In every nook and cranny a woman is sitting with a welcome on her lips. It is sensory overload. Pattaya is the land of convenience—a 7-11 every fifty feet, a pharmacy every forty feet and a girl every five feet. But it is largely a mirage to me—a town of 10,000 available women but only a few good lays; a town of so many women and so few good lookers. To some degree it strikes me as an elephant's graveyard in which old hookers come to die."

Other mongers think the quantity—and quality—are just fine. "Pattaya easily has five times the hookers that Bangkok has at less than half the price and is where experienced travelers go," writes "Nightowl2548" at the WSG. First-timers, he says, fall for "sensationalist TV reports that 'Bangkok is the Sex Capital.'" Then they "overpay so now the girls in Bangkok demand 3,000 baht [about $84] for an hour of sex when the Pattaya beer bar girls spend the night with you for 1,000 baht [about $28]."

I attempted to jumpstart conversations about the sex scene in Pattaya versus other parts of Thailand by posting the following to the various monger sites:

"Pattaya: Thailand's 'Sodom and Gomorrah'? My friend says that Pattaya is known as Thailand's wildest city. Is it crazier than Bangkok and other cities?"

In a follow-up, I asked if Pattaya pushed the envelope on "anything in particular"—kinkier prostitutes, sex shows, etc.

"Brewsterbudgen" replied, and wondered why I'd want to see a sex show. In either Bangkok or Pattaya you can have your own sex show in your hotel room, he told me. For a "wild" porno experience, he suggested Eden in Bangkok and Hell Club in Pattaya. Hopefully, one day I'll get to follow his suggestions.

Per "Khunbeng," another monger, "If you want pure debauchery then Pattaya is better. More depraved, more flesh for lower prices, everything close, sticking dildos on stage, fingering, bathtub lesbian pussy licking etc."

"Dan7373" at ISG responded in a detailed post:

"I've been to both Bangkok and Pattaya. And I couldn't stand Bangkok. Too much pollution in the air. And after some people there tried to take advantage of me, I got disgusted and left Bangkok for Pattaya. One good thing in Bangkok is that it has a lot more people, which includes more bars, more go-go places, and more massage places to have fun.

"But Pattaya is pretty good too. And it's a lot more quiet and relaxed than Bangkok. The distances between places are shorter, which means that you can simply walk from place to place. And the hotels in Pattaya are better priced and more accommodating when it comes to bringing the lady to your room for the night.

"One problem you might have in Pattaya is staying with the same lady you've arranged to show you around. Many streets there are lined with open air bars and go-go places. And you'll have to deal with many temptations, especially when you go for an evening walk.

"As long as you have a female escort, then the other ladies won't bother you too much. But if you happen to be alone in the evening, then the semi-naked ladies will be all over you. And you will have a hard time getting away, unless you choose one of them to go with you of course.

"One thing you have to be careful of is drinking too much alcohol. The ladies there are paid to encourage foreign customers to drink. And you can easily end up drinking too much, which can lead to all kinds of problems.

"If it's not a girlfriend you are looking for but a good ride, then a massage parlor is the best place to go to for that. I've been with ladies from bars and ladies from massage places, and there is no comparison when it comes to sex. The ladies in massage places are a lot better at giving their man a good ride, or two, or however many you want. And there is a good reason for it. The massage ladies tend to be a bit older, more mature, and a lot more experienced.

"A thirty-year-old lady can be just as sexy and attractive as a younger woman. But she knows a lot more about what to do and how to do it. And she is not shy about it either. If you act shy with her, then she will likely teach you a thing or two about how to enjoy your time with her. Which can be educational.

"My most pleasurable and most sex-educational experiences have been with massage ladies. Going to a massage parlor is something I recommend you do, if you want to have some real fun with an attractive woman who knows how to debauch her young horny man."

Dan7373 wraps up with a bit of health advice:

"One thing you've got to be careful of is sexually transmitted diseases. Condoms do help. But they are not 100 percent effective. Massage ladies do a lot more men than bar ladies do. And all their practice and experience makes the massage ladies very, very good at what they do. But perhaps it also makes them a bit more dangerous in terms of possible STDs."

We mongers are nothing if not practical. Nobody wants chlamydia, or worse, from an unprotected romp overseas.

CHAPTER SEVENTEEN

Ticas for the Taking

In December 2006, I went to Costa Rica for *Karma* magazine, a slick publication, now defunct, that covered nightlife (not spirituality, as one might assume from its name).

Costa Rica is one of Latin America's most prosperous countries and a magnet for eco-tourists. About a million visitors come to Costa Rica each year for its rain forest, wildlife, beaches, and volcanoes. The capital, though, San Jose, is a hotbed for mankind's favorite indoor activity. Mongers post tons of travel reports about San Jose on the World Sex Guide and other sex-travel websites. Their accounts had been enough to whet my interest in Costa Rica as an alternative to Rio.

Prostitution is legal in the country, which may help explain why 125,000 single American men take the relatively short flight there (about five hours from New York to San Jose versus eleven hours from the Big Apple to Rio) each year. Many of them seem to spend at least some of their trip in the capital relaxing with the attractive *ticas*—as female Costa Ricans are known—and women from nearby countries who have come to work in the city's thriving sex trade.

My first night, I went to the Blue Marlin bar, the epicenter of San Jose's sex scene, in the Hotel Del Rey. The bar, which overlooked a small casino (Costa Rica is a land of many vices), lived up to its reputation as a hook-up spot for prostitutes and gringos. It was around midnight, and men and women were everywhere along the counter, which undulated like a snake from one end of the bar to the other. The women were ethnically diverse, just like in Rio: bottle blondes, pouty-lipped brunettes, a handful of black girls.

As I oriented myself to the place, I had a beer with Jerry, a twenty-seven-year-old architect from Cleveland. It was his third trip to San Jose that year.

"There're girls here around the clock, but this is prime time," Jerry said.

"What about the trees and vegetation?" I joked. "Where's all that eco-tourism I heard about?"

"I just don't get all that environmental crap," he said. "I'm not here for nature hikes or bird-watching. I'm here for one thing only—screwing."

I was there to screw, too. It was fun trying to kid myself that as a journalist on assignment, I had a higher calling than the other gringos there. But the main reason I'd sought the assignment was to defray the costs of getting laid. Even if I hadn't gotten the article, the odds were I'd still eventually wind up in San Jose somehow.

A short-haired brunette approached Jerry. "You're too handsome to be alone," she said in broken English. "Let's go."

"Maybe later," he said, before turning back to me.

"She was cute," I said. "No?"

"Not really my type. Especially when there's so many to choose from."

It's a perspective shared by "Western." On his first trip to Costa Rica, he managed to mix Spanish lessons at the Costa Rican Language Academy with ample mongering.

"WOW! What a scene!" writes Western on the website www .CostaRicaTicas.com describing his initial reaction to the Del Rey. (Such exuberance seems natural for a man who signs off all his posts with "Women are like beers. I've never had one that I didn't like. Just some that I like more than others!")

"The Blue Marlin was packed and [its sister club] the Key Largo was rocking!" he continues. "I made my first attempt on a really cute tica at the BM. She was plenty friendly and spoke decent English. Of course she was stuck on *cien* ($100) so I was working the opposing side of the equation, time and service. Finally she told me that I just wanted too much and stormed off! I had been shot down by a *puta*! I consider it a good thing though. There is absolutely no reason to have to 'settle' for less than what you want. As soon as she had left another cutie took her place."

The Blue Marlin's identification with the sex trade is emblematic of prostitution's acceptance within Costa Rican society. The bar's home, the Del Rey, is a major hotel, an official tourist site recognized by the country's tourism board. The hotel even got a recommendation from Frommer's on its website which dryly noted that the Blue Marlin "is very popular with tourists, expatriates, and prostitutes." (The Del Rey's website brags that the Blue Marlin is the city's "number one meeting spot." Unlike Frommer's, however, the site doesn't hint at the purpose of those meetings.)

As long as the girls aren't minors, prostitution at a prominent establishment like the Del Rey isn't fodder for a scandal the way it might be if throngs of hookers, dressed for "work," started turning up at New York's Waldorf Astoria.

Not that the Del Rey hasn't provoked its share of controversy. A few years ago, the owners of the hotel wanted to build a footbridge to their other property across the street, the Key Largo. Like the Blue Marlin, the Key Largo—an officially-designated historical site that once housed the University of Costa Rica's music school—is a watering hole for prostitutes and mongers. It's also an official tourist site. San Jose's mayor opposed the footbridge, ostensibly because his staff didn't see a need for it. The city council, however, backed the Del Rey's proposal. The council president even went so far as to say that the mayor's hidden agenda was to discriminate against the owners because they allowed prostitution.

Whatever the mayor's reason, the council president, one of the Costa Rican capital's top politicians, had by implication come out in favor of prostitution. What a different world from the United States.

With only a few days to spend in San Jose, I planned my pilgrimage around three places with large followings on the mongering websites: the Hotel Del Rey, Bar Idem, and my hotel, the Sportsmen's Lodge.

At 2 a.m. on a weeknight, the Blue Marlin was still crowded. I was tired, but horny. A petite blonde (in overalls, of all things) came bopping up the small staircase from the casino. Most of the girls tried to outdo each other in low-cut dresses or ass-clenching skirts. But this one was cute enough to pull off the farm-girl look, even as she shimmied to Styx's "Mr. Roboto"—one of many lame eighties songs you hear everywhere in San Jose.

Her name was Tina. She wanted $100 for one hour, basically the going rate for Blue Marlin girls. I remembered all those online posts from mongers admonishing you to fight "ticaflation" by drawing the line at $75 or $80 per session, even for an all-nighter. But I was too beat for serious haggling. In any event, as soon as she noticed my hesitation, she mollified me by offering another hour at no additional cost. It didn't occur to me that I was too tired to make use of that extra time.

In fact, I was too tired, period.

Tina was as bubbly in bed as she'd been in the bar. If only I'd packed some of that Cialis I'd bought in Rio. After ten or fifteen fruitless minutes of limping along, I gave up and fell asleep. She had refused to kiss on the lips, anyway, which cast a pall over everything. I would not be one of Tina's repeat customers.

The garotas in Rio had spoiled me, as most of them had been voracious lip-lockers. A GFE is impossible for me without passionate kissing. A working girl might fuck hard enough to splinter your headboard, yet you still can't be sure that she doesn't find you repulsive. But if she kisses you right, you know there's some kind of attraction. All right, you never *really* know. But it's a lot tougher for a girl to feign fire in her upper set of lips than in her lower.

Thus with Tina, I couldn't "forget," not even for a second, that I was paying for her company.

I had similar kissless encounters with four or five working girls the next few days. It gave me a mission, though: to find a girl in San Jose whose lips weren't off limits.

Western's night at the Blue Marlin turned out more satisfying. He discusses his first romp with a working girl in his trip report:

"She was very cute with long brown hair and glasses. I strode over and broke the ice. I raised an immediate smile and I was in! 'M' is a Columbiana which went against all that I had imagined that the staunch, business-like Columbiana would be like. She is sweet, friendly and personable. Twenty-three years old, no kids, been in Costa Rica for five months. From a small town far from the city. I negotiated for two hours and we were off to the Castillo. After a shower together it was off to bed. I put some sexy Latin music on the CD player which she really liked. She is all natural and sweet in bed. She is more like a GFE than a PSE. One thing that I did find very remarkable was how small she was 'down there.' It wasn't that I had trouble with penetration but that her slit was tiny! Her whole package was about an inch and a half at most! I worked her over pretty well."

He even had a gift all ready for her.

"I introduced her to her new little friend, a mini pocket rocket, which was hers to take home. They became the best of friends very quickly! I discovered that the bed in my room 'dances' during sex. With no shoes on the legs of the bed it scoots all over the tile floor once the action starts! I don't know how many laps we made but we ended up with the bed in the middle of the room and had a good laugh! After another shower I walked 'M' to the lobby and waited with her for her taxi to arrive. Almost three hours had elapsed since we had arrived!"

Of course Western also had to concentrate on his studies. "I took a day off on Sunday," he writes. "I just kicked about town a bit and turned in at a decent hour because I had to be at Spanish school at 8 a.m. Monday."

My hotel, the Sportsmen's Lodge, was another fast-rising institution among gringos. The owner was a charismatic Californian, Bill Alexander, a Grizzly Adams type who'd made the place into a vibrant mix of mongers, wealthy American expatriates, and true outdoor enthusiasts who come to Costa Rica for activities including the country's world-class fishing, golfing, scuba diving and white-water rafting.

The bar had a regular contingent of working girls. Not as many as the Blue Marlin, but those who were there were quite attractive. The hotel was "tica friendly"—you could take the ladies to your room without having to pay a surcharge for the privilege. (As a poster on CostaRicaTicas put it: "Bill absolutely understands and supports the market of us folks who go to Costa Rica to fish for pink snapper.")

I was on the lodge's Internet terminal when a somewhat chunky girl in her late twenties sat down at the next computer. Donna was a masseuse—just a masseuse, she stressed—at a nearby hotel. She'd popped in to check her email on her way home from work. Donna had a smooth, pretty face and long brown hair. Though I wasn't attracted to her initially, her way of locking onto my eyes while we spoke won me over.

"How much for a massage?" I asked.

I didn't have enough, so we went to my room to get my wallet. The plan was to head to an ATM. But we started kissing, then groping, then fucking. I was thrilled that it didn't qualify as a massage, because there'd be no charge. Later that night, we went for dinner at a fancy Brazilian restaurant. Wow! Here I was on a date eating Brazilian food with a girl I'd just fucked. San Jose was starting to feel a lot like Rio.

Donna stayed the night, but she threw me for a loop the next morning when she asked for money, about $60. It wasn't much, especially given how much time we'd spent together. But I didn't like the fact that she hadn't been upfront about it. I paid her, but made it clear that we wouldn't be "seeing each other again."

Certainly, I'm not the only monger to have met a "civilian" girl (or at least semi-civilian, since hooking didn't appear to be her full-time job) in San Jose. Western writes on CostaRicaTicas about hooking up with one of the bartenders, "Lady 'G,'" at his hotel, the Castillo:

"I had seen her at the bar once earlier in the week but did not have the time to meet her. She is tall for a tica, slender, with long black hair and a passionate and sensual aura. Just my type! She was a working girl now working behind the bar for the first time but I was smitten. She kept reminding me that she was tending bar and not 'working.' I was fine with that. I was just having a good time hanging out at the bar. Finally, at closing time, she told me that she could not make enough money as a bartender and was quitting. Off to my room we went! WOW! She was everything I had imagined. We made a date for the next day, Monday. Monday a.m. with Lady

'G' was splendid! We took our time and really had some fun. This was the HOT Latin sexo that I was looking for! WOW!"

On the same trip, Western met a twenty-year-old who "claimed to weigh just over 100 pounds . . . but I picked her up and she was probably eighty-five pounds at most. She did have an eternal smile and a sexy look to her. I couldn't resist. We became a 'thing' for the next several days. Until Friday night when she called at 2:30 am with the RFM (Request For Money) I not only told her NO! I told her HELL NO!!"

The thing about San Jose is that there's always another girl to take the place of the old girl. A few days later, Western was at his hotel's bar when another monger's "girl showed up with her cousin in tow," he writes. "This fellow wanted to take off with his girl for a while. Would I mind buying her cousin a drink and [keeping] her company?"

The cousin, he adds, was "fresh in from Nicaragua. It was her first day on the job. Sure, I told myself. They all say that! It turns out that it was *la verdad*! [the truth]. She was eighteen years old and it was her first time [having sex] for money. She even told me later in the room that she had only been with one other man. I believe her because it showed."

Although she was a "very good kisser," Western notes "she was very timid so I took the lead and worked my way very slowly. I made certain that she had a good time. Who knows what her previous experiences had been like? I wanted her to know what real sex was supposed to be like. She really responded to my fingers and I found that I could easily get her off that way. She was a bit small and I had bit of trouble with my tongue but when on target I was able to send her up the wall that way too. When we were finished I shared my last two home-baked chocolate chip cookies with her before I took her back to her cousin."

Western's verdict on his trip? "Don't wake me up. I don't want the dream to end! That's how I feel now that I am home. . . . I'm almost afraid to go back. Might I be disappointed if my next trip does not equal this one? Is it possible to equal this trip? I guess that I'll have to find out."

He even kept tabs of his mongering "stats" in San Jose: eight sessions with four girls over ten nights. "Average price/session $67.50." The trip had also benefited his language skills, as his airport driver, the same man who'd picked him up when he'd arrived, noticed. "He is amazed at how much my Spanish has improved," writes Western. "We laughed and joked (mostly in Spanish) all the way to the airport."

About half a mile away from the Del Rey was Bar Idem, another must-see mongering spot in San Jose. Idem had a "school dance" atmosphere—"guys on one side, girls on the other," as "Prolijo" described it on the International Sex Guide. "That's actually one of the things I like about Idem," Prolijo wrote. "Don't get me wrong, I like being groped and propositioned as much as the next guy at places like the Blue Marlin, but there are times where I want to be able to just sit back, relax, sip my bottled water, chill out and leisurely make my selection without being hassled or pressured." Unlike the Blue Marlin, where you negotiated with the girls, Idem's prices were fixed at around $50 an hour during my trip.

I initially went to Idem to take photos of its girls for my *Karma* article. Idem wasn't upscale. It was comfortable, like a local pub, but with private play rooms in the back. There were about twenty girls in the bar the day I visited, some of whom were quite stunning. The manager, Roberto, was a sixty-two-year-old avuncular man with glasses and a well-groomed mustache. He couldn't have been nicer about helping me find girls who were willing to appear in the magazine. As I've pointed out elsewhere in this book, this isn't always an easy task, as many prostitutes aren't eager for publicity.

After I finished the photo shoot, I was in a quandary. It was late afternoon and I wasn't particularly horny. Was this a sign of growing old, that I wasn't instantly aroused around stunning women? Or was I just jaded? Or maybe I was worried about how much money I'd already spent in Costa Rica. Whatever the reason, because Roberto and the girls had been so accommodating, it would have felt disrespectful to leave without getting a session.

I decided to go with Marina, a lovely Nicaraguan. "Does it ever seem unnatural to be intimate with men you just met?" I asked her.

"Yes and no," she said. "This is how I survive for now, so I have to keep my mind comfortable with it. Most of the men who come here are very nice, so that's good."

"What about men you're not attracted to?" I asked.

"Everyone has something nice. Some have it outside, some inside." Marina saw part of her job as focusing on that nice quality so she "can be passionate and make him feel passion, too." It's acting, she added, "but it's not lying. Most of the men understand that this is fantasy."

If Marina radiated serenity and poise, then Diana, a prostitute I met at the Blue Marlin, was her distorted doppelgänger. Incoherent and barely able to stand, she introduced herself by groping me. But her party girl persona had a whiff of desperation. Sure enough, she told me that she hadn't made money the last two nights. I felt more protective toward her then amorous. I stroked her face, wanting to reassure her that everything would work out. But her expression turned glum, as if she'd read it as an indication that I wasn't interested in breaking her unlucky streak.

"You're very pretty," I said, hoping to lift her sprits. "There's plenty of guys here who'll go crazy for you."

It was surreal, trying to inspire a prostitute to forge ahead and find clients. I felt slimy and sympathetic in the same breath. I would have rather helped her figure out other things she could do with her life. Without the kind of inner toughness that Marina seemed to have, what chances did Diana have of surviving the sex trade intact? (One of my dreams is to set up a charity for prostitutes in Costa Rica, Brazil, and other places I've gone. There are clearly girls who don't belong in the trade. The quicker they can get out of it, the better.)

But Diana was in no frame of mind for vocational advice. I gave her $10 so she could at least take a cab home. If I were truly a nice guy, I probably would have given her more.

It's easy, however, to avoid such introspection in a town like San Jose.

Carmela, one of the regulars at the Sportsmen's Lodge, was luscious. She had silky brown hair with blonde streaks, and giant natural breasts. Unlike other girls at the hotel, she'd quash all my attempts to make small talk with her. One-syllable utterances or a bored nod were the best I could hope for before she'd turn back to her friends. This bitchy quality, of course, only made her sexier to me. I wanted to nail her in the same way I wanted to nail every hot girl who seemed out of my league. Call it my *Revenge of the Nerds* fantasy.

Carmela's friend Marta wasn't as sexy, but she was friendlier. Someone had mentioned that the two girls were lovers, so one night I asked Marta if it was true. "Very much," she said.

All right. I'd found my threesome for the trip.

We worked out a deal and went to my room. I'd finally gotten hold of some Cialis, so I was feeling quite confident. I had the girls go at each other first. Their affection for each other seemed genuine. When I couldn't take being a bystander anymore, I went after Carmela in a frenzy, pumping her as hard as I could. Sweat gleamed on her face.

I knew that all of Carmela's reactions with me were incidental, that I meant absolutely nothing to her. But in the heat of the moment she seemed quite transported. I kept hacking away at her, forcing myself not to look over at Marta. I had this insane idea that I could mesmerize Carmela with my incredible willpower and concentration. I'd heard that if you look deeply enough into a girl's eyes, and mimic the appearance of being totally in love with her, that she'll start to give way and fall for you right back. Of course, I had no real idea what I was doing. The only point of reference I had for that intense glance that's associated with being in love was the expression I'd seen on the faces of mainstream movie actors when they're being intimate, or on porn studs in action. God only knows what I must have looked like to Carmela. But she kept the rhythm and was breathing heavy, which was nice. My fantasy was that once I pulled out, she'd pull me right back in, as if she couldn't get enough of me. It had happened like that so often in Rio, where the garotas seemed to completely fall for me. Unfortunately, Carmela wasn't prepared to take the fantasy that far.

Meanwhile, thanks to the Cialis I had little desire to come. But the forty-minute session was growing short. I felt that the courteous thing to do was to fuck Marta, also. Though many working girls are just with you for the money, you still hold a part of their self-esteem in your hands, and if you don't at least go through the motions, it can hurt.

Once I started with Marta, Carmela seemed to fade out entirely, just clock-watching. She had no interest in what was going on, least of all what I was up to. My fantasy about winning her heart was a big bust. (As big as Carmela's, come to think of it.) She left no doubt when I tried to kiss her goodbye on the lips, turning her cheek to me.

It was no GFE, but it was still a nice encounter. It had satisfied at least one of the purposes of pay-for-play: sex with a gorgeous girl that you ordinarily couldn't get anywhere near. True, ultimately it means nothing. But in my mildly nihilistic view, everything ultimately means nothing. We put great emphasis on family, friends, and health. These things are crucial, but you can't take them with you. So fucking a gorgeous girl who couldn't give two shits about you is just as significant (or insignificant, depending on how you look at it). Fucking girls like Carmela is like a waking wet dream. When it's over, the only tangible thing left is bodily fluid. It's your memory of it—however you choose to spin it—that counts.

I might have had a chance at something more lasting with Allie, who was probably the hotel's only female guest at the time. I first saw her nibbling on a Danish at the free breakfast buffet, hours after all the working girls had left the lodge. A pretty Asian, Allie certainly didn't fit the profile of any other prostitute I'd seen in San Jose. But there she was, most likely hoping to generate some early-morning revenue.

"Interesting place for breakfast," I said.

She mumbled something with her mouth full. "Sorry," she said.

"No problem. What brings you here so early?"

"I was with friends that live in another part of the country. I'm flying home tomorrow. They said this place is close to the airport."

"Where are you from?"

"New York."

She was totally believable. Apparently, she didn't know that the Sportsmen's Lodge—which otherwise was a perfectly nice place, well-maintained and safe—was a male-female hunting ground of sorts.

"Where do you live in New York?" I asked. I almost spit out my scrambled eggs when she said her street: it was four blocks from my place. Wouldn't it be something, I thought, to come all this way to party with sex pros, only to hit it off with a regular girl from my backyard?

That night at the bar, I saw how truly clueless Allie was about the local sex trade. She glanced at a table of working girls. "They're so pretty," she said. "I wonder where they're from."

"You've got it a bit backwards," I said. "They're the reason that men come to San Jose." She seemed a bit stunned, but also fascinated, as I filled her in on the spicier aspects of life in this tropical paradise.

Allie and I bumped into each other the next day at the airport. I took it as cosmic encouragement to ask for her number. We went out for drinks in Manhattan that weekend. She wore a tight red dress and looked as scrumptious as any of the ladies in San Jose. When she invited me back to her house for a snack, I was sure that some of San Jose's magic had accompanied me home. Even when she spurned my advances, it didn't shake my confidence that Allie and I would end up, at minimum, having sex. It was only when she didn't return my calls, and after a month had passed since I'd so much as touched a girl, that I realized that Brooklyn wasn't Costa Rica. Or Brazil.

How could it be?

Glossary

BBBJ: *Bareback Blow Job*—Oral sex without a condom.

CIM: *Cum in Mouth*—When a prostitute allows a monger to ejaculate in her mouth. Sometimes related to the PSE (see below).

Fantamacy: The illusion or fantasy of having intimacy with a prostitute. Ideally, part of the GFE (see below).

FKK: *Frei koerper kultur*, or "free body culture" in English. Collective term for a German brothel offering other amenities besides sex, such as saunas, massages, food, and drink.

Fuckation: Taking a vacation for the sole reason of having sex with prostitutes.

Garota de Programa: Brazilian prostitute.

GFE: The *Girlfriend Experience*—Escort relationship with more direct contact; acts like your paid girlfriend, without the nagging.

Lesbiana: Portuguese and Spanish word for lesbian—also the author's contraction of the words *lesbian* and *nirvana*, describing his quest for the perfect lesbian experience.

Monger: Short for whoremonger, it's how men who travel and pay for sex refer to themselves.

MILF: *Mom I'd Like to Fuck.*

Partytreffs: A "flat-fee" German brothel. See FKK above.

PSE: The *Porn Star Experience*—Takes the GFE to a new level, with a companion who acts as your personal porn star, willing to do most anything.

PWE: The *Pretty Woman Experience*—Living happily ever after with a girl from the wrong side of the tracks.

RFM: *Request for Money.*

Termas: Brazilian hybrids of upscale strip clubs, health spas, and whorehouses.

Sexpendix

World Sex Guide (WSG):
www.worldsexguide.org
Notable sex tourism forum, frequently updated with mongers' reports from around the globe.

International Sex Guide (ISG):
www.internationalsexguide.info
Another popular online clearinghouse for mongers.

Rio Joe's Sex Travel Blog:
www.riojoe.com
The author's website.

AVN Adult Entertainment Expo:
www.adultentertainmentexpo.com
The largest gathering of the American adult industry. Held annually in Las Vegas, it's sponsored by porn trade journal *Adult Video News*.

TSM Travel:
www.tsmtravel.com
Another popular mongering forum.

Be The Mask:
www.bethemask.com
Site that gives mask-clad porn fans a chance to fuck their favorite
adult performers on camera.

Sexpo:
http://adultentertainmentexpo.com
The largest gathering of the American adult industry. Held annually
in Las Vegas, it's sponsored by porn trade journal *Adult Video
News.*

Pornweek:
www.pornweek.com
A group that specializes in creating exotic, all-inclusive vacations
with sexy porn stars.

Wan King's Partytreff Club Guide:
http://partytreff.thumblogger.com
Guide to Germany's pay-one-price brothels, where for a flat rate
you can have sex with all the girls you want.

Top 100 Adult Vacations:
www.top100adultvacations.com
A site dedicated to bringing you information on independent
agencies and escorts, complete with a long list of sex tourism
destinations.

ClubHombre:

www.ClubHombre.com

An online discussion group and information exchange between "seasoned veterans and excited newcomers"; targeted toward the single adult traveler seeking "excitement (sex), adventure (sex), and some of the most beautiful women (sex) the world has to offer."

Frankfurt Sex Guide:

http://frankfurt.usa-sexguide.com/bordellolinks.htm

Guide to brothels in Frankfurt, Germany; includes maps, standard prices, and other advice, with further links to more than a dozen Frankfurt brothels.

Nevada Sex Guide:

www.travelsexguide.tv/nevadabrothels.htm

A site with links to over forty brothels (legal in Nevada), escort services, strip clubs, and the like.

TSM Travel:

www.tsmtravel.com/09

The Single Male Travel 2009 Update; allows members access to articles, photos, and movies of other members' experiences. "You don't have to be young, handsome, or rich to be with a beautiful woman. . . . A big smile, a good attitude and not being afraid to make some blunders along the way is all that is needed."

ABOUT THE AUTHOR

JOE DIAMOND HAS WRITTEN FOR VARIOUS PUBLICATIONS, including the *New York Daily News*, *TV Guide*, the *New York Post*, *Newsday*, *Maxim*, *Hustler*, *Fox*, and *Oui*. He's currently a writer for Playboy TV's new travel series, *69 Sexy Things to Do Before You Die*.

A former aide to Rudy Giuliani and a former public policy advocate, Diamond created ParoleWatch, the nation's first website providing public access to detailed information about violent felons, about which the *New York Post* commented, "[T]ireless activists like Joe Diamond of ParoleWatch have succeeded in turning parole reform into a national issue." Diamond's many television appearances include *Hannity and Colmes*, *Geraldo Rivera*, and *Hard Copy*, and news segments on CNN, MSNBC, Court TV, and the Fox News Channel.

Diamond has a degree in journalism and political science from Brooklyn College.